a sweet romantic comedy

CW01464816

Never
Happens
on
Valentine's
Day

FRANCESCA SPENCER

Dedicated to my lovely New Zealand whanau, with love and gratitude.

Chapter 1

Lydia

"You just don't know who is going to walk through that door." I wave a yellow gerbera in the direction of the hotel entrance. "He could be pulling up right now, as we speak. You just don't know what the universe is going to provide for you, Sheena. Or when." I pop the slender green stem in its place among the other blooms in my floral arrangement in the lobby.

Sheena pretends to be busy with a booking, her eyes glued to the computer screen at the reception desk. "You're such a romantic, Lydia."

"No, I'm not. I'm the opposite. But I do think that, even though we live in a small town, exciting, beautiful romantic things happen." Sheena rolls her eyes at me, then returns her attention to the booking or whatever it is she's pretending to do. She types officiously, brisk and noisy, and huffs. "They do," I say, emphatically, in response to Sheena's negative huffing. "And I know, because I've seen beautiful romantic things happen with my own eyes."

I guide another gerbera stem into the large round clear glass vase, where it joins its siblings, along with asters, ferns, and the glorious golden trumpets of Canada lilies. I stand back and appraise my work. It's almost complete. Stepping to one side and then to the other, I make sure there is harmony and balance from every viewpoint.

"Are you going to tell me about Molly and Cam... again?" Sheena raises her eyes from the screen and fixes me with an arched eyebrow.

"I don't need to, do I?"

"No."

"My point is, Sheena..." I extend my arms wide for emphasis. "... to be open to possibilities." I drop my arms and turn my attention back to my grand floral statement.

"Let's face it. You work in a hotel, so you get to meet all sorts of interesting people."

"People who are passing through. Not staying. Here for a few days. Then they're gone." Sheena tidies the reception desk with swift efficient movements. She gathers some loose A4 printed papers together with both hands and taps them into line, short end on the flat desk surface. "Also, I am a professional. There's no way that I would entertain the idea of romantic entanglement with a guest of The Oak River Hotel. That's a no-no. Uh-uh." She shakes her head and leaves through a door with a 'Staff Only' sign. "Tut-tut."

Although Sheena doesn't say it out loud directly, she would very much like a boyfriend. I sense these things. We chat. I listen and I pick up on things said and unsaid. For example, "A woman does not depend on a man for her happiness," clearly means, "I'm happy at the moment but wouldn't it be nice to share that happiness with a significant other?" Or, "Being single is so much easier than being in a relationship. I only have myself to consider," means, "My life is so ordered and boring, I'd love to have someone mess it up a little." These casual snippets of conversation are tell-tale signs of a woman who is longing for a partner. But Sheena would never admit to it.

I had the same feeling when Molly, my best friend, got together with Cam, the new fire chief in town. When something wonderful happens, it spills over and affects everyone, and Sheena became hopeful and optimistic that something that wonderful might happen to her.

But as time has gone on, I feel her optimism ebbing away. Which is a shame. I'd like to help out. Find Sheena a handsome beau. I'd like to see her happy and perhaps walk down the aisle to a gorgeous groom who is waiting for her at the altar. I picture the kinds of flowers that would adorn the church at her wedding. I go through some mental petal color-swatches in delicate violets and cornflower blues.

But of course, the final floral design depends on the time of year. Each season comes with its own challenges and triumphs. Would it be a summer wedding? I could do something fabulous with sunflowers! Yes.

Images of Sheena's wedding bouquets and reception displays grow and morph, expand and shrink in fabulous Technicolor arrangements in my head, until a hot pink pompom dahlia that is being less than cooperative, snaps me back to the lobby of The Oak River Hotel. The flower needs gentle but firm encouragement into position. I tussle one stem in front of the other, between trails of ivy and wisteria, until they eventually behave and stand obediently where they're supposed to. I turn the vase and measure the height of another deep red dahlia before adding it to the glorious firework burst of summer color. Stepping back to assess my finished creation, I'm pleased with another fragrant welcoming stand of blooms on the reception desk of The Oak River Hotel.

"Howdy ma'am," a tall stranger touches the brim of his cowboy hat. He then removes it and holds it in his hands at his chest. He waits at a respectful distance from me. "I have a reservation." His voice is low and deep, which makes me think of smooth warm caramel sauce drizzled over vanilla ice cream. The resonance of the man's voice is a soothing balm on my senses. If that voice, with its distinct southern flavor, filled a bathtub, I would happily step in and submerge fully.

Instinctively my eyes sweep from the hat, covering the man's chest, down to the cowboy boots he's wearing, then back up to his head topped with tousled light-brown hair. Casually, he combs his fingers through it, from his forehead in a fluid backward sweep. A gesture that is so compelling, I can't look away.

The man with the hat smiles and says, "Maddox's the name. Luke Maddox."

"That's so nice," I say mesmerized by the man's intensely blue eyes that crinkle beautifully in worn creases at the outer corners. His eyes are the color of the morning sky when you look straight up. They are the color of infinity. Of translucent light. The blue of the glittering ocean's surface with untold mysterious depth beneath. They are eyes that gaze at a distant horizon in the haze of summer's heat and glare of winter's snow. They are watchful eyes. Kind eyes. They are patient. These eyes will look out for you. Will keep you safe. He will search for the one he loves and won't quit until he finds... me. Me? That can't be right. I cough slightly. "Hi. I'm Lydia," I say, finally finding my voice and shaking my mind into activity. "Lydia Lane." I step out from behind the floral display.

"Lydia Lane." Luke Maddox passes his hat into his left hand and extends his right out in greeting. "That's a mighty pretty name, if I may say so."

"Thanks." My cheeks color up and I wonder if the heating has been turned on.

We shake hands and I'm on the point of asking if he's a real cowboy, or pretending to be one, and if he's going to a dress-up party, when Sheena appears from the door behind the reception desk.

"Good afternoon, sir. How may I help you today?" Sheena says with professional courtesy.

Luke Maddox releases my hand and darts his sparkling blue eyes across the reception desk to Sheena's bright welcoming smile.

He nods a greeting. "Maddox. Luke Maddox. I have a reservation for tonight, ma'am."

"That's right." Sheena beams. "Welcome Mr Maddox." She lowers her gaze to refocus on the computer screen. Her fingers click the mouse a couple of times. The printer purrs to life and a piece of paper slides out.

"How was your trip, Mr Maddox?"

"Oh, fine. Fine. There was only a minor delay in Orlando between flights, but otherwise, it was okay."

"Well, welcome to Oak River. I'm sure you'll have a pleasant stay." Sheena expertly retrieves the sheet of printed paper and smooths it out on the counter in front of the cowboy. "Just sign here," she says drawing a little 'x' before handing her pen to Luke Maddox.

I watch carefully because I think I know what's going on there. I have a nose for such things.

The little 'x' is a dead giveaway. It's a kiss, of course!

Ah, Sheena. Yes. I think we've found just the right man for you.

"How long are you planning on staying in Oak River, Mr Maddox?" I say this casually, as I would to any visitor, handsome or otherwise.

Luke beams an arc lamp smile which hits me with a surprising physical force. Lightning, or something similar, blinds me for a second but it's not an unpleasant sensation at all. My limbs have turned to jelly, and strange joyful voices sing in my head, *Hallelujah!* The only thought I have is, Gosh. Luke Maddox, you are absolutely gorgeous.

"I'll be here at the hotel until tomorrow. My family has recently acquired Green Acres Ranch. Do you know it?"

Sounds familiar, but I can't place the name until Sheena says, "Oh, yes. It's the Dixon's place, up there on the national park road, isn't it?"

"Yes, ma'am."

"I heard that the Dixons sold up and moved on after Mr Dixon Senior was admitted to a care home," says Sheena. "I think the family members all live in Richmond now."

"Yes, well. The land is prime horse country," says Luke Maddox. "Horse breeding is our business."

"Oh, how exciting!" I say enthusiastically.

"Do you ride, Miss Lydia?"

"Oh, no. I mean, I can sit on a horse and let it take me around, but I'm under no illusion that I have control of an animal that's just so big and powerful."

Sheena shoots a raised eyebrow glare at me that says, clear as day, *Back off. He's mine.* I pack up my craft knife, secateurs, and wire into my toolbox. I can take a hint. And that is exactly what I predicted. I giggle to myself - teehee - at my cleverness.

Luke Maddox nods and smiles again and adds his signature to the piece of paper next to Sheena's kiss. I know his name ends with an 'x', but could it be interpreted as a kiss right back?

Chapter 2

Luke

The friendly receptionist, Sheena, shows me to my room, overlooking the town square. The room's furnishings are unremarkably adequate, yet comfortably unpretentious. There's an old-world charm that reminds me of my grandparents. The bed is the only piece of furniture that looks recently updated. Inside of fifty years, or so.

I walk over to the window and take in the scene of small-town goings on. Although I'm far away from my home, there's a familiarity to the town square layout. The hotel, like the town's square, has retained a feel of yesteryear. The grand exterior of carved stone columns and pediments speaks of a proud past, rather than an ambitious, go-getting present. Civic buildings opposite, and a library on one side, are adorned with similar sculpted architectural features, that seem too grand for such a small town.

A pleasant formal flower garden, with benches and triangles of grass, occupies the communal area below my window. Pathways crisscross through the gardens, connecting one side to another, and meet at a central fountain.

Oak River in its heyday must have been quite different from the sleepy little town it is today. It has retained a quaint dignity, like a strait-laced old lady who still thinks it necessary to put on her Sunday best for church.

"There are towels and a robe in the bathroom, here." Sheena opens the door to show me, then closes it again. She indicates a red leatherette folder on the polished wooden desk with Welcome embossed in gold letters on its cover. "Here's where you'll find local information and a brief illustrated history of the town and surrounding area. Oak River was an important export hub when the river was navigable. And it was instrumental in the story of the conflict for independence. The townsfolk are very proud of their heritage." She hands me the room key. "It's a shame that you're too late for the Annual Spring Fair. It was last weekend. You've just missed it."

"Oh yeah?"

"It's very popular," says Sheena with a generous smile. "And so much fun. The local Historical Society performs a battle reenactment that's very authentic, with original firearms and outfits the soldiers and rebels would have worn."

"Sounds interesting." I pick up the leather-look binder and let it fall open randomly.

"Oh, it is." Sheena claps her hands together and holds them at her chest as if she is praying. "If you'd like to read more about it, it's all there in the Welcome folder."

"Alright." I casually flick through the pages and dividers not really taking in any information. Then I lift my gaze back to the receptionist and say, "Thank you, Sheena. You've been very helpful."

"No problem. And please do let me know if I can be of any further assistance, at all," she says, smiling as she walks to the door. Stepping through, she reaches for the handle to close it after her, but pauses to say, "Oak River is a small town with a big heart, Mr Maddox. I'm sure you'll feel at home here in no time."

"Thank you, ma'am. I'm sure you're right."

As the door clicks shut, I recall the pretty woman who was hiding behind the huge vase of flowers in the lobby. What was her name? Something pretty. Lydia. That's right. Lydia Lane. I'd like to find out more about her. But first I have some business to attend to.

I call the land agent and local lawyer to confirm the appointment we have set up to sign the ownership papers for the handover of Green Acres Ranch. Then I call my dad to let him know I've arrived and that things are going according to plan.

"Great news, Son," my father says on the line. We talk about the horses and the list of excited customers who are lining up, with their checkbooks ready, to purchase stock from our breeding program. Our award-winning American Quarter Horse stallions and mares are world-class. "I have every confidence in your abilities regarding the new ranch, Luke. No doubt about that."

There's a pause and silence on the line. I walk to the window and watch townsfolk in the square.

"I'm hearing a 'but', Dad." I sit on the bed.

"Yes. Well. You know we talked about increasing our online presence."

"Uh-huh. Yes." I wait for my dad to continue.

"Maisy has volunteered to update the website and explore social media opportunities." My dad's words snap out in quick succession like rapid gunfire. He's excited. Me? Not so much. I gaze out of the window again. "Isn't that great?" he says.

"Is it?" My heart sinks.

To say that Maisy, the youngest daughter of my older brother, Darryl, is a handful, is a massive understatement. Because we're relatively close in age, she's always been more like an annoying kid sister, rather than my niece. And, since we grew up in the same house, the irritating kid sis thing was amplified to the max.

She stole my stuff. She had no respect for anyone or anything. Maisy's probably the reason I spent so much time in the stables with horses, just to get away from her. Then, I moved out of home, as soon as I possibly could.

Maisy is the dictionary definition of rebellious. She was kicked out of two schools and almost didn't graduate from a third.

With hindsight, my brother's parenting skills were probably at fault. He indulged his little princess with everything her heart desired and subsequently created an obnoxious monster. Maisy.

"Now. Luke." My dad's tone has changed to default: authority. "I know what you're thinking."

"Mmmm. Do you?"

"Yes. You're thinking that Darryl is off-loading Maisy on you for some free babysitting."

"Isn't that what's going on?"

"No. Maisy has grown up. A lot. She's very career-focused these days. And, I believe, she's going to do a great job." I suck in air through my clenched teeth. I'm searching for a way out, but I'm backed into a corner. "Luke. Be nice. Okay? She's going to start here at the home ranch, then when you've settled in, she'll come and take some shots of the breed horses and facilities there. Alright?"

I grunt. But I don't say anything. Even if I did object, I'd just be overruled, so I keep my mouth shut. But my mind flipflops back in time to relive the moment Maisy screamed off down the road in my car that she'd hotwired, with her badass buddies, and my credit card that she used, without my knowledge, across three states at various gas stations, liquor stores, and motels. It was quite The Bender.

"She's coming there to help you out, Luke."

"Alright, Dad." I breathe into the handset. "I get that I need help with the tech, but how else do you imagine that Maisy could possibly help me?"

"You never know, Luke. Maisy's had her wild time, but I think she's turned a corner. She's got some new friends now. She's not hanging out with that loser she was dating. What's his name? Oh, never mind. Anyway, the point is, she needs the credits for her university paper, and we can benefit and get all that Friendbook, Tactic, and what-have-you, for nix. It's a win-win. Don't you think?"

"Sure, Pa. Whatever you say."

"That's my boy. And, Luke, she knows she's got to prove herself. She's a Maddox, after all. If she plays up. You just send her packing. No one's going to judge you for that. You're the boss there, okay?"

"Okay."

As I hang up the call, my good mood deflates. The last thing I want is to be a babysitter for my brother's wayward brat. Maybe she has changed. It's been a while since I've seen Maisy. I'll try to keep an open mind. However, I'll keep my credit cards and cash locked away from her sticky little thieving fingers.

Chapter 3

Lydia

At the library, my good friend, Molly arranges books and other relevant items on the display table. This month's theme is Nature and Outdoor Pursuits, with a focus on what to do and see in and around Oak River. I stopped by to see if she had time for a coffee, and also because I wanted to ask if she had any insights concerning Sheena and the new cowboy in town.

"She hasn't mentioned anything to me," says Molly holding the green cut-out card title in place on the pin-board.

"No. Me neither. It's just that it's been at least a month since he moved onto the ranch." I huff audibly as I pass Molly a brass thumb tack from a jar I'm holding. She secures the 'O' of Outdoor.

"Well, they're both busy," Molly says as I hand her another brass tack from the jar. "But I'm sure that, if they like each other, they'll get around to connecting." She thumbs the tack into the letter 'P' of Pursuits. "Eventually."

"Do you think he's called her?" Another tack for the 'N' in Nature. "Do you think she has called him?"

"Gosh, Lydia. Maybe Sheena believes in taking her time; in letting things just happen… naturally."

"Well, it's not like they're going to run into each other in the street." I put down the jar of tacks on the table. "Let's face it, things are not going to just happen 'naturally' unless they are made to happen 'naturally'." I smooth out the creases in the topographical map of the national park that Molly plans to pin to the board under the title. "Events leading to an outcome need to be coordinated and orchestrated beautifully, if they are going to occur naturally."

I like the soft colors of the map and the way the contours of the ups and downs of the land are depicted with pleasing concentric lines at varying distances from each other. My finger traces the road from Green Acres Ranch, which is marked by a collection of haphazard squares denoting farm buildings, to Oak River town center, and the library indicated with the label *lib*.

"Are you planning something?" Molly asks with a quizzical smile.

"Who me? No. Not at all."

"Remember the song, 'You Can't Hurry Love'?" Molly applies dots of glue to the back of the map.

"Yes, but..."

"I know your heart is in the right place, Lydia, and you just want to see people happy..." I help Molly stick the map on a large sheet of brown paper.

"Yes. That's right. I do. And I think I have an instinct for spotting potential love birds."

"Like me and Cam?"

"Exactly. I was right about that, wasn't I? You knew, as I did, that Cam was The One for you."

"Well, yes, I did. Eventually. But I had this very bossy friend who insisted that we were perfect together." Molly fixes me with a mock-serious stare. "So, I really didn't have much choice." She holds up the map, stuck to the reinforcing backing paper, and pins it to the board. "So, what makes you think that this eligible cowboy is interested in Sheena?" Molly steps back to survey her efforts. She seems pleased.

"Just a feeling." I pick up a book about tree species and flick through the informative pages. "Also, when I was in the hotel with fresh sunflowers, just the other day, Sheena started telling me about her new kitchen renovations. Then we were chatting about her single status. And I asked, in a roundabout way, how long it has been since she last went on a date, and if there was, perhaps, someone that may be of interest to her romantically." I close the tree book and return it to the display table. "Sunflowers last very well even in summer heat." My friend listens patiently. "Sheena didn't tell me directly that she has her eyes on a special someone. But she kind of went all sparkly and said something, in passing, that gave me a little hint that maybe... And I'm not getting my hopes up, but she said that there might be a certain someone who has made her reassess her single status. Of course, I tried to probe for more details, but our conversation was interrupted by a guest in the lobby, so I cannot confirm my suspicions at this time." I feel like a detective solving a case. "Could it be a coincidence that Sheena's new positive outlook regarding romance, has something to do with Mr Tex walking into her life like John Wayne?"

"Alright. It's possible, I suppose."

"Yes, Molly. I thought so too." A library visitor enters so I drop the level of my voice to a whisper. "So, I said to myself, 'Lydia, this is your latest challenge.' Here are two very attractive people who need a helping hand getting together."

Molly laughs quietly and tidies up loose pieces of string, tape, and left-over colored cardboard. "And what makes you so sure they want to be together? Were they flirting?"

"Sheena was professionally courteous, and he called her ma'am."

"Is that it?"

"No," I say edging closer to my friend. "Sheena drew a little kiss on the check-in paper."

"Are you sure she wasn't just showing Mr Cowboy where to sign his name?"

"Mmmm. You could be right. But I watched how they interacted and I'm sure there was some kind of chemistry. You know, a spark."

"Okay." Molly appraises her display. "Well, he might already be taken."

"No ring. I checked his ring finger for evidence. Nothing. Not even a tan line."

"That doesn't mean anything." Molly laughs. "How about this idea. He could be interested in you. Have you thought about that?"

"No! No." I blush, although I'm not sure why. Perhaps it's because I remember Luke Maddox's incredible blue eyes and the slow, easy way he spoke, and the way he looked in jeans.

Molly smiles and says, "Maybe it's your turn, my friend. How long has it been since your last date?"

"Who me? Nah." I tut. "I don't date. Huh. Anyway, I'm far too busy and sensible for anything the least bit romantic. I am the fairy godmother and never the Cinderella. That's just the way it is."

"Never say never, Lydia." Molly winks at me. There's a beat and then she says, "Ah, yes. I was going to ask. Are you going to Dylan's gig next Friday?"

"At The Old Oak?"

"Yeah. Should be a fun night. The band has been practicing some new songs. We should go."

"Great. Yes. I remember Star Rangers' last gig. It took me a good few days to recover after that night. Phew. We danced so much."

"Sshhhhh," hisses Molly reminding me that I'm in the library. "Keep me posted on developments regarding Sheena and the cowboy, okay?" she whispers as she hurries to where an older woman, with a stack of books, is waiting by the counter.

"Absolutely. You'll be first to know when I get called upon for wedding arrangements."

Chapter 4

Luke

Green Acres Ranch is impressive. I liked the way it looked on paper and the website, but now I'm here, checking out the stableyard, the paddocks, and the tack room, the prospect of running this place is daunting but, equally, energizing. The property, of course, is not solely mine. It belongs to Maddox Holdings, our family's company, but this division is effectively mine to manage. I have been entrusted to turn Green Acres into a profitable business to add to our already extensive portfolio of horse breeding ranches and farms, mostly located in Texas.

The responsibility weighs heavy on my shoulders. I have a lot to prove. And a lot to live up to. But I've been working with my dad and my brother, Darryl, and I feel confident I can apply what I've learned from them, over the years, right here. And I don't feel as if I'm doing this on my own. My dad and Darryl are only a phone call away, but I'm in charge. I'm the boss here. It's time for me to step up. And I'm ready.

After signing the legal papers, I took over ownership and moved in a few weeks back. I already feel at home in the no-nonsense white weatherboard farmhouse.

The stable staff are competent and helpful. All of them wanted to stay on, which is great, as I don't need to advertise for new employees. Ray, the stable manager, Amy, Georgia, and Saskia seem happy with me as their new boss.

I haven't made any major changes yet. I want to observe the systems to see what's working before I step in with my ideas. It's important to develop trust with people you work with, to get the best from them. I'm taking my time getting to know the staff. They need time to get to know me too. I think I'm fair and approachable although, it's true, I prefer animals to humans.

Horses are my passion. My dad said I could ride before I could walk. He gave me my first pony, Spider, when I was four. I have a photo of me riding him bareback. I must have been eight years old when the picture was taken. No reins. I'm hanging onto Spider's mane with one hand. The other hand waves my hat in the air, and I'm yahooing at the top of my lungs. I remember the feeling. It was caught when the photo was snapped. Absolute joy. And I still get that same buzz of being on horseback, even now.

Although my buddy, Spider, is long gone, I still love horseback riding. Just being around horses makes me happy. So, I feel blessed to be born into a horse-loving family and blessed to be living my dream of running an American Quarter Horse stud farm.

I've never had a regular job and never wanted one. I don't feel like I'm missing out. Although days are long, and work is physically hard, I never tire of being on a ranch. There's always something that needs attending to, fixing, or sorting out. I can't imagine anything else I'd rather be doing. I was born for this life. And now I have a ranch of my own, I couldn't be happier.

I lean on the fence behind the homely wooden house, that's now my home, and look back up the meadow to the shadows of the trees beyond. Horses graze the lush grass lazily in the sunshine. Their tails swishing happily.

Alright, I could be happier. Part of the reason I put my hand up for the Green Acres Ranch project was for a fresh start after my fiancée, Courtney, called it quits. She decided that she'd changed her mind, or her heart, about me and our future together.

We were childhood sweethearts, and I always thought that we'd walk down the aisle someday and run a farm and have about ten kids. But a little while ago, I'm not sure when exactly, she started acting strange. Distant. I didn't really pay much attention because I thought she needed space. So, I left her alone.

Maybe I shouldn't have left her alone. Maybe I should have paid her more attention and... Anyway, one day I picked her up to go out for our date night. We sat side by side in the truck. I drove to our favorite bar and tried to be upbeat, talking about this and that. She couldn't look at me and when I asked her what was on her mind, she started to cry and said she didn't want to marry me anymore. I pulled over because it felt like she'd hit me in the face. The world spun around, and I was dizzy. I felt nauseous. My whole future, everything I thought was rock solid - for definite, carved in stone - just crumbled away in a nano-second.

When I eventually opened my mouth and told her what she meant to me and how we were going to be so very happy together, she shook her head and said she was sorry. She opened the cab door and got out. She said she was leaving for Los Angeles in the morning and there was nothing I could do or say to change her mind.

I was numb. For a long time. It was hard to be in a place that Courtney and I had shared since we were kids. To be there without her, surrounded by painful reminders, well, it took its toll. I didn't want to go out. I didn't want to see anyone. I felt guilty for not being enough for her. I felt as if I'd let her down. Her leaving me felt as if it was all my fault, no matter what my friends said. I was not in a good place. Thank goodness for family. And horses.

Ray coughs politely at my shoulder to get my attention. I turn slightly to hear what he has to say. I like my stable manager. He's a no-nonsense kind of guy. Quietly spoken. Good with horses.

"There's a young lady just arrived." Ray glances in the direction of the house. "Says she's your niece."

"Oh, man. She's early," I say, perplexed, as I stride down the track to the farmhouse, followed by Ray.

Maisy is waiting on the front porch. "Hey, Uncle Luke! How-the-devil are you?"

"Maisy. You should have called." I climb the steps. "I was planning to come get you from the airport. Tomorrow."

"I know. But sometimes I just want to go it alone." Maisy hugs me warmly. "Make my own way, you know." She steps back and looks up at me and grins. "Surprise you. Are you surprised?"

"Yes." But not in a good way.

"So, I got an early flight, caught a bus from Richmond to Oak River, then hitchhiked most of the way out here, and walked the rest." Maisy glows with accomplishment. "It was a mission, but here I am." She sings, 'I am' musically, with three notes, like a radio jingle.

"Yes. Here you are." Maisy's arrival has thrown me.

"It pays to travel light." She pats her small compact backpack that leans against the porch railing, beams her high-wattage smile at me, and then directs it at Ray. "And who's this handsome fella? Aren't you going to introduce me, Luke?"

Ray tips his hat and smiles shyly.

"Maisy, this is Ray. He's my right-hand man around here. Ray, this is Maisy, my niece. She's going to be helping out with digital something-or-other that I don't understand."

"Nice to meet you, Miss Maisy," Ray extends his hand in greeting.

"Ha. You can drop the 'Miss'. I'm just Maisy." She shakes Ray's hand energetically up and down. "And I'm here to put Green Acres on the map." Maisy releases Ray's hand and hoists herself up to perch on the porch rail. "Luke. I have a lot of ideas for this place that could turn up revenue tenfold."

"Okay." I fold my arms. "How about you unpack first?"

Ray says something about checking in on Treasure, the new mare at Green Acres. She's a beauty and hopefully pregnant. "I hope you have a pleasant stay, Maisy." He tips his hat and turns to leave.

"Ray." I call after him. "Perhaps you could take Maisy for a ride and show her around, if that's alright with you?"

"I'd be happy to." Ray tips his hat again before striding away to the stables.

Maisy watches him go then says, "Ray. He seems like a nice man."

"Yes. I believe he is. Now, I'll show you to your room. It's pretty basic but it has what you need." I move to pick up Maisy's backpack, but she swats me away and heaves it onto one shoulder. Then she follows me into the house. "Just tidy up after yourself, okay?" The flyscreen slaps shut behind us. I lead my niece up the stairs and show her into the room at the back overlooking the horses in the meadow and the hills beyond.

"This place is wonderful, Luke. Grandpa said I'd love it up here. And he's right." Maisy dumps her pack on the pale pink paisley bedcover.

"But you know that this is just temporary, right?"

"Duh. I have to get back to Austin to hand in my final project, so don't worry, Uncle Luke. I'll be gone before you know it." She sits on the bed beside her pack, bounces playfully a couple of times, and shoots me a goofy grin.

"Right. Listen." My voice is level but stern. "My dad believes in you, so I do too."

"Sounds like it from the welcome I'm getting." Maisy huffs and looks out of the window.

I ignore her sarcasm. "Take your time. Unpack. Settle in. Then come and find me at the stables, okay?"

"Sure." Maisy twists her nose to one side as if assessing her options. I turn around to leave and I'm about to pull the door shut behind me when Maisy says, "I have some great ideas. I can really help out here." I pause to listen in the doorway. "Luke."

"Yep."

"I've changed."

"Good."

31

In the stableyard, Ray is with Deedee, our prize stallion at the ranch. He is a legend. His official stable name is Delaware Delmont Dandy, but he's affectionately known as Deedee. He's getting on a bit in years, but he's still at the top in horse breeding circles. Genes don't get old. We've stockpiled Deedee's little necessities, packaged up on ice, for the right mare at the right price. He has offspring in every continent, from Tokyo to Dubai; Melbourne to Joburg; Mumbai to Versailles. Deedee's colts and fillies are global and I'm proud about that. And I'm proud to be the engineer of horse love. Although love doesn't have anything to do with it.

As I stroke Deedee's powerful neck, I can't help my mind from wandering. Maybe it's being away from the family homestead, but I keep thinking about the pretty woman at the hotel. I shake the thought away. I've got too much going on here for any romantic notions.

But it would be nice to see her again, socially. Casually. I could stop by when I'm next in town. We could have coffee, maybe dinner. Nothing serious. Just friends. I could bring her out here. Maybe she likes horses. We could ride up to the lookout at sunset, maybe. That would be nice.

I walk out of the bright sunshine into the dim stable. Treasure stands patiently as Ray pats her flank. "She's in foal alright, boss."

"Great news," I say relieved, excited, but also a little worried, as if I'm about to be a parent. "I'll call the vet to come and give her a once over."

Chapter 5

Lydia

L aura and Marty, my team at Blossoms in Bloom, are busy finalizing a celebrity wedding that we are designing in a few weeks. We're going over orders and who's doing what. My team is brilliant. I'm so thankful to have them working with me.

I've proudly built up my business from a humble florist store, selling floral arrangements, to a wedding planning and floral design service, that I love. We have bookings into next year, which is wonderful. Having staff in store means I'm free to organize, get out to see clients, and visit venues. I also work with Kate at The Half Moon Café who is my go-to wedding cake creator. We often coordinate design elements so that the chosen wedding themes follow through in a multi-level extravaganza.

The celebrities getting hitched soon are Rita Carmichael, ex-model, and Brodie Kent, ex-quarterback star for the Boston Bullets. They're both locals who went away, got famous, then came back. Theirs is a love story worthy of the best romance writer. They are perfect together and, surprisingly, I had nothing to do with it. But I was thrilled and delighted when they came in one day, holding hands, and said that they'd love it if I designed the flowers for their wedding.

I had a brief consultation at the Carmicheal homestead. They have a date locked in for early Fall. We discussed themes and the general feel they wanted to create. They said they just wanted something lowkey and intimate in a marquee on the back paddock. The couple outlined a rough budget but, basically, left it up to me. What a dream job!

I'm so excited. I want everything to be perfect. Not that I want everything to be less than perfect for a non-celebrity wedding. But the publicity, even for a small lowkey event, will be wonderful exposure for Blossoms in Bloom.

The next step, after the initial consultation, was presenting Rita and Brodie with a mood board of colors, textures, and sketches for sculptural installations for the ceremony. They went for my ideas one hundred percent and loved the autumn themes of soft russets and reds; ochres and yellows; grasses and seedpods.

The hero element of the design is numerous fruit-bearing branches of the crabapple tree. It sounds unlikely but the humble crabapple, as decoration, is stunning. The colors of the tiny apples vary from deep red to golden yellow. They're like natural Christmas baubles, round and shiny. And perfect for weddings because, according to folklore, they are a symbol of fertility and represent love and marriage. Rita, Brodie, and Rita's parents loved my idea of a harvest feel that would be fitting and beautiful in the rustic farm setting.

I like to work with Nature and source local whenever possible. So, lucky for me and the happy couple, there are crabapple trees on the Carmichael property.

"It makes sense to go with what's available," I say gleefully as I'm shown the crabapple trees in the Carmichaels' kitchen garden. "These are wonderful. There's no point in making things expensive and difficult by ordering spring flowers in October, or tropical orchids from Singapore when you have a showstopper like this growing right here on your property."

Of course, the only exception to my 'seasonal and local' rule is Valentine's Day. Everyone wants roses. In February. It's mad but we do it. Valentine's Day without roses? Not possible.

At Blossoms in Bloom, my laptop is open, and I run through the spreadsheet labelled Rita & Brodie. Laura sits opposite me at the counter looking at the same document on the iPad. Marty is making up a bouquet order for pick up later in the day.

"I'll leave the checklist to you, Laura."

"Yo." Laura looks up from her screen briefly.

"Go through the orders, cross-check with the suppliers." I glance down the color-coded columns.

"Got it."

"If anything doesn't add up, we need to get on top of it now," I say as I reach for a pencil and jot down 'orange' in my notebook. "If a supplier can't deliver flowering ginger, then ask what else they have in orange, asap, so I can give the clients the option of going with another idea. Also, if they are offering a special, grab it. We can do a whole orange store theme. What do you think?"

"Sounds good," says Laura as she scribbles a note on her pad.

Usually, my suppliers are reliable, and usually things go to plan. That's because I am fastidious. I check and double-check.

"Just one more thing," I say with seriousness. Marty and Laura stop what they're doing and look at me with concern as if I've spotted a problem. "The store looks and smells incredible. Thanks, team."

Laura and Marty relax instantly and continue what they are doing. I wander around my store, thinking about Rita and Brodie's wedding, then stop to admire the window display. Laura and Marty have done a fantastic job with a rusty wheelbarrow overflowing with summer blooms. Flowers and leaves spill out of the tops of a pair of rubber boots, and an old-fashioned watering can seems to be sprouting a riot of chrysanthemums. I love it. Flowers make me smile.

The string of bells at the door announces a customer with a pleasant tink, tink, tink. Sheena comes in looking slightly harassed. She has an emergency order from the hotel.

"It's a fiftieth wedding anniversary," Sheena says breathlessly. "I know that you're super busy, but the daughter has booked her parents in as a treat. Last minute because of health issues. I said I'd ask, on her behalf, if we can get something gorgeous for their room."

"I think that would be okay. When are they checking in?"

Sheena glances at her watch, then says, "Thirty minutes."

"Okay then. What did she have in mind?" I close my eyes as if I'm a medium summoning spirits at a seance. "No. Don't tell me. Roses. Red. A dozen."

"Yes!" says Sheena, surprised. "How did you know."

"Trust me. I've been in this biz for some years now." I move to where a pail full of rose bouquets, made freshly this morning, stand ready for sale. "These perhaps?" Sheena nods, so I find a simple round glass vase and arrange the bunch of twelve red roses, offset with delicate white gypsophila, and leatherleaf ferns. "When you add the water in the room, sprinkle this sachet." I hold up a sealed white packet. "It helps prolong the freshness of the roses." I turn the vase and tweak the stems to make sure the arrangement works from every angle. "Would you like to choose a card?"

"Great idea," says Sheena approaching the array of greetings cards at the counter. She picks one out and writes a message inside, then puts it in the envelope. I punch a hole in the gift card and thread a piece of raffia through, then tie it onto one of the roses. "Just gorgeous!"

"It smells wonderful too," I say leaning across the counter and fixing her with a knowing look. "So, Sheena." She meets my gaze and appears slightly alarmed. "Has he asked you out yet?"

"Sorry?" Sheena furrows her brow. "Who?"

"The Texan. The cowboy, of course."

Sheena starts to laugh. "No. What are you talking about?"

"You can't tell me that you don't think he's handsome."

"Yes. I suppose he is, in a southern rodeo kind of way."

"Ha! I knew it. I knew there was something in the air besides the fragrance of gladioli." I retrieve a cardboard carton from under the counter.

Sheena shakes her head and laughs. "You've been watching too many Hallmark movies. Or perhaps you've designed too many weddings."

"No, my friend. I have an instinct for getting things going in the romance department." I use tape to reinforce the sides and bottom of the carton, then I place the vase of roses inside. "Just look at Molly and Cam." I pick up the carton and walk toward the door.

"Wow, Lydia. I didn't realize you were Cupid in that love story," Sheena says as she follows me through the store past shelves and buckets of flowers and leaves. She then walks quickly past and opens the door, making the string of bells chime again.

"Not so much Cupid, but it was me who pointed Cam out to my idiot best friend." I carry the roses out to Sheena's car.

"So, you think that Luke Maddox is into me?" Sheena looks skeptical but places her hands over her heart.

"Stranger things have happened, Sheena. Leave it with me. I'll do some digging for you."

"Okay then, if you want," says Sheena climbing into the driver's seat still looking unconvinced.

"Sure. No problem," I say as Sheena starts the engine and winds down her window. "I'll charge these to the hotel account?"

"Yes, please. Just reference my name. And thank you so much," Sheena says with a smile. She blows a kiss then drives away.

I wave and watch as Sheena goes. Another happy customer. I love my job.

As I walk into my store again the phone rings. "I'll get it," I call out as I reach for the handset next to the till. "Blossoms in Bloom. How may I help you today?"

Rita Carmichael is on the line and sounds worried. She tells me that the crabapples at her folks' place have developed some kind of blight.

"Oh, Lydia. I'm sad," says Rita. "The fruit is all mottled with black blotches which looks horrible. We're going to have to rethink the floral design without the crabapples."

"That's such a shame." I hold the phone away from my head while I think. "Listen. It's not over yet. We can still go with the crabapples but from somewhere else. Crabapple trees are not unusual. I'm pretty sure I can source them from someone locally. It might alter the budget a little, but…"

"I don't mind. If you think you can find healthy beautiful crabapples, then do it. I'd just love to have what we agreed on. I don't want to compromise anything on our special day."

"Alright, Rita. I'll see what I can do and get back to you tomorrow. I'm pretty confident we'll get our gorgeous little apples."

"You're the best. Thank you." Rita hangs up the call and my head whirs with possibilities.

"Crabapples!" I say loudly to the flowers in my store.

Marty pops his out of the storeroom. "Did you call?"

"No. But yes. Crabapples. Marty. Who grows crabapples around here?" They're not an item commercially grown, that we can order from our regular suppliers. I only used them in my design because they were so abundant on the Carmichael property.

Marty scratches his head, then he says, "The Dixon ranch had an orchard and I'm pretty sure there were crabapple trees. But it's been sold now, so…"

"Yes. Marty. You are a genius." I grab my assistant by his shoulders and kiss his cheek. "Two birds. One stone."

"Lydia?" Marty looks concerned.

"Yes."

"Are you okay?"

"Marty. You have no idea how okay I am." I scoot around the counter and grab my purse, then I head for the exit. "Can you mind the store? I'm going out to see a cowboy about some apples."

Chapter 6

Luke

"So, Uncle Luke," Maisy says relaxing on the couch with a mug of steaming coffee in her hand. She gives me a crooked sideways smile that suggests she's cooking something up. "Have you met anyone... interesting while you've been here?"

"Sure. Mr Schnider, the lawyer in town, was very helpful with the paperwork and handover."

Maisy makes a non-committal noise, something like a short hum, as if I've just suggested that she wears coveralls to her high-school prom. Or the answer I'd given her is just plain wrong.

She twists her nose to the side and says, "That's not really the interesting I was talking about, Luke."

"Can you expand on your thought process? Or am I expected to read your mind?" My laptop is open on the table in front of me, but I'm not focused on the rows and columns of the spreadsheet.

"You are hilarious. And Dad was right. You don't have a clue. I've lost the bet."

"What bet? What are you talking about?"

My older brother Darryl, Maisy's dad, is the golden boy. The favorite. And I suppose, because of our age difference - I was a happy accident, according to Mom – I've felt as if he's always looking down on me. Aside from splitting up with Courtney, I'd say that part of the reason that I volunteered to run the ranch up here in Virginia, was to be far enough away from Darryl, and my dad, to do things my own way.

My brother and I are poles apart. Total opposites. I know horses. I've always wanted to be around them. Darryl? He'd rather be driving the business. He's smart and ruthless. He doesn't mince words. And he's not particularly bothered if he upsets people who get in his way.

Maisy is her father's daughter. My guard is up when she's around.

"Let me spell it out for you," Maisy says, laughing. "Have. You. Met. A. Nice. Lady... Yet?"

"Is that all you think about, Maisy? I have a horse farm to run here. My day is full, from the moment I wake up in the morning until the second I lay my head down to sleep. There is no time. And, I mean, no. There's nothing left for... courting."

"Ah. Aren't you the sweetest man?" Maisy's laughing at me and it's my turn to roll my eyes to the ceiling. "Quaint. That's what you are. And, you know what? Some women go mad for quaint. Especially quaint with a Texan accent." Maisy scoots to the edge of the couch, puts her mug on the coffee table, and picks up her phone. Her thumbs are a blur as she types something. "Let me see now," she says as if she's forgotten that I'm still in the room.

"Are you planning our Open Day?" I ask knowing full well that she isn't.

"Nope." Her eyes scan the screen.

"Okay, well, if you don't need anything, I'm going to check on the horses." I close my laptop and stand up.

"Just hold on one second." Maisy raises a finger which has a hypnotic effect on me and keeps me from reaching the door. "I'm creating a profile for you."

"A what?"

"Username. That's you." Maisy's eyes flick up briefly. "Luke M. Password. Profile name. Lonesome Cowboy. Capital L. Capital C."

"Maisy. I have things to do. I've got no time for games."

"This isn't a game, Uncle Luke. This is TheOne4U dating app."

"Excuse me? Maisy." I'm too perplexed to follow up with a sentence of cohesive thought. All I can do is pace and rake my fingers across my scalp. My niece has been in my house for less than a week and already I'm wishing she was on a plane heading south. Or anywhere.

"Don't be such a technophobe. This is the way people meet people these days."

"I'm not a technophobe. I embrace technology that helps me in my day and makes my life easier. What I object to are things that take away my attention from what's important."

"I think that loneliness is an important issue, especially among men in rural communities." Maisy doesn't look up from her screen. "I can show you the stats of depression and suicides if you want. And besides..." She shoots me her goofy grin, "... this is fun."

"For you, maybe. But honestly, I can't see it working out for me. Turn it off, please." I change down my tone to something softer. "I'm not going to use it. I appreciate you wanting to match me with someone... nice. But if someone is right for me, they'll walk right in. I don't need tech for that. When I meet The One, I'll just know. So, please..." Maisy looks at me, her head tilted to one side. "Turn it off." I fix her with a stony look. "Now."

"Oh. Alright. You're such a stick-in-the-mud." Maisy crosses her arms and sinks back into the couch like she did when she was seven years old.

"Maybe I am." I don't want to be negative. I want to get along with Maisy. She has some good skills that I don't have. I'd like to keep things amicable between us, so I say, "I'm going to the stables. I've got stuff to do. But when I get back, how about you show me your ideas for the ranch."

The mood in the room changes in an instant. Maisy sits up like she's spring-loaded and grins at me. Her sparkle returns. "I thought you'd never ask!"

There's nothing at the stables that needs my urgent attention. I just need to get outside and move around. I'll ride Deedee to the back of the property through the trees. I just felt suddenly claustrophobic in the house, ambushed by Maisy and her online dating app.

If I'm honest, I still feel sore about Courtney leaving. Rejection is a bitter pill to swallow. I know in my head that she left through no fault of mine, but in my heart, I still go over all the things I could have said and done to make her stay. The same internal conversation goes around and around my brain and just gives me a headache. She wanted to go. She didn't want me anymore. You can't make someone love you if they don't.

I take my hat from the coat rack in the hall and put it on as I stride to the stables.

Deedee neighs a greeting and kicks hello on the door of his loose box. Treasure and the other horses are out grazing in the paddock, and I know that the stallion feels as if he's missing out.

"Don't worry boy. We're going out. Just you and me."

Ray is in the tack room where he's polishing the saddles. He tips his hat when he sees me. We have a brief exchange about horse feed and orders of oats for the winter. I tell him that I'm taking Deedee out. I grab his bridle from the peg on the wall and heave his saddle from the rack.

"Enjoy your ride."

"Thanks, I will."

Then I carry everything out to the stableyard where Deedee tosses his magnificent head and shakes his rockstar mane. I sling the saddle over the stable door then let myself in. He nuzzles my hand with a warm velvet nose. Despite his size, Deedee is a gentle and good-natured soul. Although he lets Ray ride him, I have a special bond with this horse. I wouldn't say he's mine. We're more like buddies. Someone I can talk to. Someone who understands me. Who doesn't judge.

"Stand still while I get you saddled up, boy." Deedee paws the ground and tosses his head a couple of times.

The well-polished saddle leather creaks softly as I hoist it onto Deedee's back. I fasten the girth straps and fit his bridle, gently pulling his ears through, one by one, before buckling it up behind his cheek.

I grab the reins and lead the stallion out of the stable. His hooves plod rhythmically on the paving outside. Then I pull the reins over his head, reach up and grasp the front of the saddle, put my foot in the stirrup, and swing my leg up and over. Deedee adjusts his stance to accommodate my weight. I collect the straps of leather in my hand and squeeze gently to encourage the horse to walk on.

The horses in the paddock sense our presence. They whinny and prance as we walk by. I kick Deedee into a trot on the dirt track leading up to the treeline and the ridge beyond. It feels good to be riding. It always feels good to be on horseback. It clears my head. I release Deedee's reins and kick him into a full gallop. He loves to run, and I just let him go. We charge up the hill to the lookout, then slow to a stop. I gaze down the sweep of the valley to the ranch buildings that look like models in a mini landscape of meadows, hedges, and trees. I breathe and feel better about everything.

After my ride, Deedee takes me back to the stableyard. I jump down and lead him into the loose box where he has clean straw, water, and a bag of hay and oats, a measured meal of all the vitamins and minerals a stud stallion needs to stay in peak condition. I take off his saddle and bridle then use a body brush to groom his coat in broad sweeps across the contours of his muscular flanks. I comb out his mane and tail. He seems to enjoy the pampering.

"There now. Fit for another trophy."

I smooth my hand flat along Deedee's white blaze down his handsome face when a female voice interrupts my action.

"Hello, there. Mr Maddox? Is that you in there?"

I step out into the sunshine, shielding my eyes against the glare. "Hey. I'm Luke Maddox. How can I help you?"

As my eyes adjust to the brightness outside, I see who the voice belongs to, and I'm stunned for a minute. A warm smile washes up from my toes and spreads across my face.

"Hi, I hope this isn't an inconvenient time, Mr Maddox."

"No. Not at all." I'm suddenly shy, aware that I'm probably covered in hay, straw, and Deedee's hair. "Lydia. It's Lydia, isn't it?"

"That's right." Lydia's bright intelligent eyes meet mine. "You remembered."

How could I forget? "What can I do for you today, ma'am?" I say opening the stable door and coming out into the yard. Lydia walks closer.

"Mr Maddox. What a beautiful horse." Lydia looks past me to where Deedee is munching his feed.

"He is, isn't he. This is our stud stallion. Top breeding sire with all the American Quarter Horse pedigree papers. His official name is Delaware Delmont Dandy, but we call him Deedee, for short. It should be Dee-dee-dee, of course, but that's a mouthful too."

Lydia laughs. "Dee-dee-dee sounds like you're singing a tune. He's handsome alright." She gazes admiringly at my horse, then says, "Well, I don't want to take up your time. I know you must have a million things to do, but I have a request concerning your crabapple trees."

"I didn't know I had crabapple trees."

"Well, you do, and they look very healthy and productive. The apples are in good condition, displaying a variety of colors, and they hang in manageable clusters. And I'd like to... Mr Maddox."

"Luke."

"Luke. I have a wedding coming up and the whole design is around crabapples. I have a vision of creating an archway from crabapple bowers for the ceremony."

"Sounds wonderful."

"Yes. It's going to be amazing. The only problem I have is the crabapple trees I was going to use have been struck with an ugly blight, so I was hoping to use some of yours."

"I don't see a problem with your request at all. I didn't even know I had crabapple trees on the property, so I guess whatever you want is fine." I think for a moment. "How about you show me the trees you're interested in."

Lydia and I walk down the driveway to the fence line at the road. Small trees with branches covered in tiny round fruit form part of the thick hedge border. Lydia walks up to the nearest one and smooths her hand over the red and orange fruit.

"Look, they're perfect," she says smiling at me with impish joy. Then she tells me when she'd like to come and cut the branches. "The wedding is a few weeks away, so these teeny tiny apples will be a teensy bit bigger but not as big as normal apples you find in stores."

"Okay. Come and get what you want whenever you like."

Lydia seems more than happy with my comment. "Well, that's wonderful. I can work out an offer. The couple have a generous budget for floral design."

"How about we just call it a wedding gift. I mean, I didn't even know I had crabapple trees. And I didn't even know that crabapples had a value. So, this time, whatever you'd like, take it." I smile. "But next time, we'll work something out. I could be sitting on a potential untapped goldmine of crabapples."

"That is so nice of you, Mr Maddox."

"Luke. You can call me Luke."

"Okay. Luke. I'd love to add you to my list of suppliers, if that's alright."

"Absolutely."

Lydia's eyes sparkle. I seem to be hypnotized by her smile, and I can't move away.

Neither of us speaks for a while, then Lydia says, "How are you enjoying living here in Oak River?"

"It's fine. The horses are happy so that's all that counts, really."

"Have you had time to meet people in our community? We're quite friendly and approachable."

"I'm sure you are." We walk a few paces back to the house.

"So, there's a local band, Star Rangers, playing at The Old Oak Bar & Grill next Friday night," says Lydia. "They're pretty good. They play covers. Mostly rock. Indie. Old-school mostly. Nirvana, Foo Fighters, No Doubt, Johnny Cash. I'm just thinking about the songs I like the best. You should come. It'll be fun." She stops walking. "And you'll meet people."

"Thanks, Lydia. I'd like that," I say although I'm suddenly shy about seeing Lydia in a social situation. I look down at my boots. "Would you like to come in for a coffee or tea, or something cold, perhaps?"

"Ah, thanks but I've got to go. Another time maybe? But thank you so much for helping out with the crabapple supply chain."

Lydia reaches out to shake my hand. Polite. Business-like. But her touch sends a rush through me giving me instant goosebumps that I hope she doesn't see. She turns and walks briskly down the track to the gate.

"I'll see you next Friday," I call after Lydia as she walks away. She gets into her van. Then she waves to me as she drives off.

I can't believe I have a date. A date with a very pretty, attractive woman who asked me out. I'm dizzy with anticipation. I haven't felt like this since high school. I calm my fluttering heart and walk back to the house.

"Who was that?" Maisy asks when I enter the living room.

"We met at the hotel."

Maisy makes her low humming noise again. She doesn't say anything but flashes one of her annoying crooked smiles my way.

"What? Why that look?" I say, instantly defensive.

"Just... she's pretty."

"Is she?" I'm trying to sound casual. I don't even want to have this conversation, but I ask anyway, "How could you tell from in here?" The last thing I want is my niece nosing around and trying to organize my love life.

"Yes. Luke." Maisy fixes me with a stern glare then punches me and laughs. "She is very pretty. Now, sit there and listen to my ideas. We are going to start pony trekking here."

"Oh yeah?"

"Yeah." Maisy grabs her laptop and pushes me down into a chair. "Here's why. Number one. No one else is doing horseback rides within a twenty-mile radius of this cute little historic town. I've done some digging and, although Oak River is a small town, it's a popular weekend destination for residents of Richmond. And the Annual

Spring Fair brings a big crowd from further afield. So, the conclusion is, that the potential spending public doesn't reside here permanently but comes here for leisure activities. Such as hiking in the national park just up the road."

"Interesting."

"Yes. Number two. Here are some figures, sales projections, and potential earnings from horseback riding and treks." Maisy opens a color-coded spreadsheet. "These numbers here are worst-case scenario. Let's say we get two people a week who want just a one-hour ride. And then, this is potentially what we could get if we offer lessons, treks, family and group rides." She clicks through to the next slide and traces her finger along an upward-slanting line on a graph. "The beauty of this is simplicity. We have the horses. We have the land. Ray took me through the woodland to the lookout point. It is amazing. I took some shots for the website. Look." Maisy scrolls through landscape images on her phone. "What do you think?"

"Sounds great. No. Really. I am genuinely impressed." Maisy beams at me. "I can't believe that no one else is doing horseback rides out here. Maisy. Make it happen."

"Really?" My niece looks suspicious. "You're not going to argue with me?"

"No. Do you want me to?"

"No. I just thought that whatever I came up with, you were going to knock down out of principle."

"That's ridiculous. And you obviously have a very low opinion of me."

"Does that mean I can go ahead with TheOne4U dating app?"

"No. And don't push your luck."

Chapter 7

Lydia

The hotel lobby is dim compared to the summer sunshine outside. Sheena is at the reception desk in conversation with an older couple. I walk over to the floral arrangement to check for wilting foliage, while I'm waiting for her to finish. I pull out some daisies that are past their best and tug the remaining stems around to fill in the gaps made by my extractions. In a few minutes, I hear Sheena wish the couple a pleasant afternoon. They walk toward to door. I seize my chance and approach the desk.

"Hey, Sheena. How are things going?"

"Lydia. It's not Thursday already, is it?"

"No. I'm not here for floral design reasons." I check that no one is going to interrupt before I continue. "You remember that gorgeous cowboy who stayed here a few weeks ago. His family bought the Dixon place."

"Yes. Of course. A charming man."

"Charming and handsome, as I recall."

"Is he?"

"Yes. Sheena. You said so yourself. Gosh. You surprise me." I check the hotel entrance half expecting Mr Luke Maddox to suddenly appear again. "You haven't seen him, lately, have you?"

"No, Lydia."

"He hasn't stopped by... socially?"

"Not that I know of..."

"Oh," I bite my lip and think. "Well, come to The Old Oak next Friday."

"I can't come out on Friday," Sheena says without taking her eyes off the computer screen on the reception desk.

"Why not?"

"Because I'm getting a quote for my kitchen renovations." Sheena mouths the words making very little sound, as if it's a secret. She looks down at the keyboard for a minute, then back to the screen.

"On a Friday night?"

"Yes." Her eyes flick up at me for the briefest second, then back to the screen.

"But Luke Maddox will be there. I went to see him at Green Acres because of the crabapple situation."

"The crabapple situation?"

"Yes. Blight has ruined the Carmichaels' crop that I was planning to use for Rita and Brodie's wedding."

"Oh."

"Anyway, Mr Maddox. Luke has some wonderful crabapple trees. Just gorgeous. And he's so kind. He said that I was welcome to take what I needed. No charge. Isn't that nice?"

"Yes. That's a very generous gesture."

"So, while I was up at his place sorting out the key design element."

"Excuse me. Sorry, Lydia, I'm lost." Sheena sighs audibly.

"Crabapples! The key design element for Rita and Brodie's wedding."

"Right. Yes. Of course," Sheena says looking back to the computer screen.

"Well, while we were chatting, I invited Luke along to the gig on Friday night, and I told him that you'd be there,"

I say emphatically even though it's a little untrue. "He's coming to see you." This may be an outright lie.

Sheena stares straight ahead, then turns to me and says, "Now, Lydia. Do you think that you're getting a bit carried away? Tell me exactly what Mr Maddox said."

"I said that Star Rangers were a pretty good band and they're playing next Friday, and he should come and meet some people."

"So, he didn't say specifically that he wanted to see me."

"Alright. No. But it was implied." I smile broadly. "I've set it up for you. All you need to do is, come along looking fabulous, and, voila!"

"Oh, I don't know Lydia. I've already arranged for Gary from Gary's Kitchens & Bathrooms to come and have a look at my pipes. He's so hard to pin down."

"Sheena. It's Friday night. Let your hair down. Live a little." I dance around in front of the reception desk. "It'll be fun. And it's not like a 'date' date. It's a social mingle. A testing-the-waters, kind of thing. And I'll be there as your wingman. No worries. And remember the last time Star Rangers played? It was awesome."

"I didn't go," Sheena says while she types. "I think I may have been working or something."

"Well, you missed out. They were brilliant and I'm predicting that this time they'll be even better." I check the time on my phone. "We should see them before they get snapped up by a major label and their ticket prices go through the roof."

"Well, I suppose I could reschedule."

"Gosh, then Sheena, you are in for a treat. Not only will you have the attention of a hot cowboy, you'll get to hang out with me, and we'll have the best dance. What do you say?"

"Alright. But I'll probably come later... after the kitchen consultation."

"Great. That's brilliant," I say collecting the discarded bits from my floral display and making sure I have everything before I leave. "It's going to be fun."

I leave the hotel and wander over to see Kate at The Half Moon Café. I need to check on arrangements for the celebrity wedding and also, I need a coffee. A strong one. I'm perplexed by Sheena's lack of enthusiasm. I set her up on a date with the handsomest man in town and it's as if I've asked her to do my yearly accounts. I don't understand it. If it were the other way around, I would be champing at the bit to get close to that swoony cowboy. A bristle of indignation causes me to stomp out onto the sidewalk.

Crossing the square, I stop, take a deep breath, and notice how beautiful the formal gardens are this year. The rose bushes are at peak bloom, and clumps of elegant blue and white agapanthus nod wisely and tell me to slow down. They're right, of course, so I ease my pace.

"Lydia!" Kate greets me from the counter at The Half Moon. It's late afternoon and she's getting ready to close up for the day. "Perfect timing," she says. "I'd love your take on the decoration for Rita and Brodie's cake." She disappears through a door into the back kitchen and I wait at the counter, scanning the empty café tables. When Kate comes back, she's holding a tray of delicate pansies and violas. "These are the ones you brought in for me when we were talking about colors and themes. They've been freeze-dried."

"That's so clever. They still look so fresh and colorful."

"So, I was thinking... It's going to be a three-tier carrot cake."

"Yum."

"Maybe I'll use a whole heap of the petals on the top layer, then kind of spread them out on the bottom two layers, as if they've been tossed and they're floating down onto the cake. And look." Kate holds up two orange butterflies made from feathers on thin wire. "These will look like they're flying around." She beams at me. "I like the idea of something a bit fun; something non-design-y, if that makes sense. Rita is such a nature-girl. I think she'll love this."

"Absolutely." I admire Kate's handy work. "You know her best. When is she coming to see it?"

"She's not. And that's why I needed your opinion. She trusts me to make her wedding cake the best it can be. A wedding cake that'll be perfect for them."

"No pressure, then," I say, making Kate laugh. "I'll put together some table arrangements with pansies and violas." I take out my notebook and write, 'order pansies – R&B's W'

She takes her tray of decorations back out to the kitchen and calls out, "Do you want a coffee?"

"Yes. Please. But only if you have time?"

"Sure thing. Go ahead and lock the door. And please, turn the sign around to say Closed. I love closing up early. It makes me feel as if I'm being a bit naughty. But if no customers are here, I'm allowed."

"What will the boss think?"

"Haha. She's okay, I guess, because she's me!"

I settle into the corner table out of sight from the street. It's the couple's table. It's the table in the café that's private. Perfect for dating.

"I've sourced some crabapples," I shout across the café to Kate who is at the coffee machine.

She turns toward me and holds up an index finger, then shouts back, "One minute, Lydia. I can't hear what you're saying." I watch as steam clouds form from the milk jug. Soon Kate comes over with a cup and saucer in each hand. "I thought you might like a biscotti, too." An elegant slim almond biscuit sits on each saucer. "I'm trying a new recipe. Let me know what you think."

"Thank you."

"What were you saying? Something about apples?"

"Ah yes. Rita called to say the crabapple trees at her parents' place have blight. We needed to rethink the floral displays or find other healthy crabapple trees. So, I found some."

"Good for you. Where? Not far, I hope."

"Not at all. It was Marty's idea. He really is such a help." I dunk my biscotti into the cappuccino foam. "Green Acres."

"The Dixon's ranch?"

"Yes."

"The place was sold, wasn't it? Bought by some Texan horse breeder."

"That's right. Maddox. Luke Maddox."

"Lydia. You're blushing."

"It's the coffee. It's hot." But as I say these words I know I'm lying. An image of Luke Maddox's broad shoulders and shy smile occupies my frontal cortex. The shadow across his face from his hat. His relaxed easy posture. Ah yes, the cowboy swagger.

"So great. We have crabapples for the wedding. I'd love to include a few on the top of my cake."

"Perfect. That would tie everything in beautifully." I sip my coffee and take a moment before saying, "And I've set Sheena up with Luke Maddox. On a date. They're going to the Star Rangers gig next Friday. Are you coming? Should be good."

"Gosh, Lydia. You are a force of matchmaking. Is this a side hustle you're getting into?"

"Ah, no. I just like to see people happy. And when I spot a guy and a girl who look great together, I'm not averse to giving them a little helping hand." I sip my coffee. "Sheena has been, you know, single for a while. So, when Luke Maddox turned up, I just put two and two together. Joined the dots."

"Exciting."

"I think so. But Sheena doesn't share our enthusiasm. I thought she'd be over the moon about seeing Luke 'Handsome' Maddox at The Old Oak, but she was so ho-hum about it."

"Perhaps, Lydia, she doesn't think he's as handsome as you do."

I huff. "He's not just handsome, he's nice." I lean back in my chair. "When I asked him about the crabapples he just said, 'Take what you want, any time'. Isn't that nice?"

"Are you sure he wasn't flirting with you?"

"No." I laugh. "I'd know if he was." My reverie is interrupted by someone tapping on the café window. It's Dylan, Rita's brother. He cups a hand around his face and peers in. "I'll go," I say standing up to let him in.

"Hey, am I late?" Dylan walks in holding a toolbox.

"No," says Kate. "Sorry, Dylan. It was quiet, so I just closed up early." Kate turns to me and says, "Dylan's been so kind helping me put up new shelving in the kitchen. It has been on my to-do list for yonks."

"No problem, Kate. Anything for you. You know that," Dylan says with a warm smile. "And this week's good. I don't have a trail booking, so I can be your handyman."

Kate smiles then turns to me and says, "Since Rita decided to desert me and go off and get married, Dylan has been my best friend." She turns her attention back to Dylan. "I swear this place, and this person would fall apart without you."

Dylan laughs and begins to walk toward the kitchen, but he stops when I say, "Hey, I'm looking forward to the gig on Friday."

"Cool. Me too. We've learned some new songs. Well, new old songs," he laughs. "We're doing some Nirvana, Chilli Peppers, and G.N.R."

"Are you going to play any slow songs?" I ask.

"What?" Dylan tilts his head with inquiry and puts down his toolbox.

"You know... romantic type of songs so people can, you know, get close and slow dance."

"We weren't planning on it. Star Rangers like to rock out." Dylan plays air-guitar.

"Yes. True. But don't you think it might be nice. For a guy to grab a girl?"

"Everywhere around the world, like 'Dancing in the Streets'?"

"Exactly!"

Dylan thinks for a beat, then says, "Do you know what. We weren't planning on having it on the set list, but I'd love to play 'Always' by Bon Jovi. It's a great power ballad with an awesome guitar solo." He plays the solo on his air-guitar for a minute. "Yeah. We don't usually do requests, but I think the guys would be cool working that song into the show."

"Ah, perfect." I put my hands together in prayer position. "Thank you, Dylan."

"No problem. I think you're right. We should mix things up a bit," Dylan says as he picks up his toolbox in one hand, his air-guitar in the other, and walks away. Once in the kitchen, we hear him singing the lyrics to the nineties classic.

"Are you up to something, Lydia?" says Kate leaning across the table.

"Who me? Nah. I just like to encourage love, wherever possible."

Chapter 8

Luke

Maisy booked a flight south. The deadline for her final project is looming and she needs to return to her university in Austin to submit all the elements in a presentation. I'm more than slightly relieved that our time together is up. I offer to give Maisy a ride to the airport as I can't run the risk of her missing the plane and showing up again at my place.

"Thanks for putting up with me, Uncle Luke," she says outside the sliding door to Departures. "You're not as bad as I thought you'd be."

"And what does that mean?"

"Oh, you know. Boring."

"You think I'm boring?"

"Well, yes. While I was staying with you, you didn't go out once. You didn't take me out and introduce me to anyone." Maisy kicks the paving in pretend five-year-old behavior. At least, I think it's pretend.

"Maisy. It may have escaped your notice but I'm running a ranch here. My time is taken up with ranch stuff."

"You still gotta live, Luke." Something in Maisy's words strikes a nerve. I open my mouth to refute the charges. "You're not getting any younger."

"If you must know, I'm going to a gig in a bar this Friday," I say defensively, but I'm instantly self-reproachful for rising to take her bait. "If you were staying, you could have come with me."

Maisy smiles, then reaches her arms around my neck in an awkward hug. "Next time. We'll go out for sure, next time I'm here. If I'm invited."

"Of course." I smile despite myself. "There'll be a next time."

"Well, thanks for the ride to the airport."

"No problem. I had to make sure you got your flight otherwise..." I shrug but I don't finish the sentence. We laugh. Then, when the mood settles down, I say, "And thank you."

"For what?"

"For getting the trekking material together and organizing the Open Day. That was a great idea."

"I'm not sure you'll be able to run it properly without me," Maisy says folding her arms across her chest.

"I'm not sure either, but I'll have to."

"Just assign someone the task of taking photos. They'll look good on your social media pages."

"Ah yeah. I hadn't thought about that."

"See, Luke." Maisy rolls her eyes at me. "You need me here."

"I'll be okay." I hug Maisy again. "You're going to get an A plus for your project, I am sure about that."

My niece glows with pride for a minute then she says, "Right. Gotta go." Maisy grabs her backpack and scoots in through the automatic sliding doors before I can say anything more.

I wave through the glass, but I can't see Maisy. She's gone. It feels as if I'm waving at my own reflection.

ele

Friday night comes around fast. It's been a while since I went to a gig in a bar. Since Courtney left for Los Angeles, I haven't even wanted to go out. I didn't go out in Austin because I didn't want to run into our friends and be confronted by that conversation that always begins, "Hey, I heard about you and Courtney and I'm really sorry. You were perfect together." Something like that. Anyway, it's refreshing to be in a new town where no one knows me. And I don't know anyone. At least not beyond polite chit-chat.

I park the pickup in a side street and wander into The Old Oak Bar & Grill. The building is a rustic barn construction with bare wood beams open to the ceiling, and original wooden floors. Beyond the bar, where people are ordering drinks and talking together, a makeshift stage is at the far end of the large open-air courtyard. Background music plays a sound bed beneath chatter and laughter. The place is filling up. There's a buzz of anticipation as people take their drinks to tables outside. I wait at the bar, order a light beer, and survey the crowd.

There's a friendly vibe. I lean my back against the wooden wall beside the bar and drink my beer. I suppose it's still early. I wonder when Lydia will arrive. After a few sips, there's an eruption of noise from the crowd as band members take their place on the raised stage. They wave to the crowd and each test out their instruments. The background music is turned off.

"Hello Oak River!" the frontman yells into the microphone which complains with screeching feedback. The audience pauses conversations, raises glasses and bottles, and reacts with appreciative thunderous shouts and whistles. "We're Star Rangers," the singer says to an enthusiastic roar. "And this is 'Smells Like Teen Spirit'."

The guitars scream and the drummer bashes out the Nirvana classic. I forget that I'm here on my own. All focus is on the stage. I relax and enjoy the music. Then, out of the corner of my eye, I spot Lydia coming in. She's smiling and chatting to some others. She sees me and waves. I wave back. She comes over to the bar with her friends. The music is too loud to have a conversation beyond hello. But we stand close together and occasionally she looks up at me and smiles. The next few songs are rocky and loud too. I like the energy. A few people are dancing up at the front.

"Thank you, everyone," says the vocalist. "We're going to take a short break. But don't go anywhere."

The crowd from outside surges in and surrounds the bar. I'm immersed in loud voices ordering drinks and raucous drunken laughter. Everyone is having a good time.

"They're great, aren't they?" shouts Lydia only just discernible above the din. I lean toward her. Her eyes twinkle.

"Yeah. I like their song choice. Thanks for inviting me. I'm having a great time."

Lydia nods. "Excellent. Come and meet some people." I follow Lydia to where a group of people are standing in a close knot. The conversation stops when Lydia says, "Hey, everyone. This is Luke Maddox. He's new in town so please make him welcome. Introduce yourselves. Go."

Everyone laughs then, one of the women whom I recognize from the café in town says, "Alright let's start with me. I'm Kate and I own The Half Moon Café."

"That's where I've seen you. Great coffee by the way."

"Thanks. I think so too."

The next person is Cam. He's the town's fire chief. He's standing next to Molly, his wife, who works at the library.

"She doesn't just work at the library. She's lying," interjects Lydia. "She manages the library. If Molly wasn't there, the place would quickly fall into ruin."

"Ah, Lydia. I love you," says Molly laughing.

"It's true!" say Kate and Lydia together. Cam hugs his wife, then reaches for her hand which he raises to his lips. He kisses her fingers gently as if it's the most natural gesture in the world. Something about their intimacy causes a wince of pain somewhere in my chest. I swallow hard to shake off the discomfort. What is it I'm feeling? Envy? Loss? Loneliness? I don't know.

Lydia surprises me by linking her arm through mine. I'm surprised but it's not an unpleasant sensation. Does she sense my mood? I'm not sure. But the familiarity of her arm in mine makes me feel safe, as if she has caught me and stopped me from falling. I want to hold her hand like Cam is holding Molly's, but that would be weird when we hardly know each other.

"Sheena should be here soon," says Lydia releasing my arm. "She'll miss the second set as well, if she doesn't hurry up."

"I'll call her. See where she is," says Kate who finds her phone in her purse then steps out of the bar.

The guitarist from the band joins our circle. Lydia leans close to him and says something.

"Hey, man. I'm Dylan," he says grabbing my hand in a wrestle while bumping my shoulder. "It's good to know you, bro."

We talk about the band for a while. Dylan says that he's fairly new to Star Rangers. "I've been playing guitar for a few years, but only in my bedroom. It's fun to get out and perform in front of a friendly crowd who don't mind if I go wrong." He laughs. "Hey, where's Kate?" Molly says that she's calling Sheena outside because it's too noisy in the bar. Dylan nods. "Okay, just so long as my number one fan is still here," he says as his attention shifts to the stage where the other band members are getting ready to play again. "I'd better go. Nice to see y'all. And please, get up the front and dance, will you?"

Kate comes back shaking her head. "Sheena's on her way," she says.

Lydia relaxes a little. "She's missing out on a really good night."

The conversation stops there because Star Rangers' vocalist, says, "Alright everyone. All you people who have been sitting down here relaxing, your time is up." He strums a raucous chord which reverberates through the bar as he holds up his guitar to the audience. "It's time to party!"

"Come on," yells Kate. "Let's get close to the band for a dance."

The women squeal and thread their way between the tables and find a space in front of the stage. Cam shakes his head and laughs. His eyes follow the funky females, but he stays where he is, against the wall. The bar is clear, so I buy another drink, then join Cam. The band is into another song when Sheena arrives.

"Hey!" she yells above the music. "I made it."

"Good to see you," I yell back. Cam raises his beer bottle in greeting. "Can I get you a drink?"

"No thanks," Sheena yells.

The music is way too loud for further conversation. So, we stand next to each other and watch the band and the audience enjoying themselves. I can just pick out Lydia and her friends, illuminated by colored lights, jumping around somewhere near the stage.

Chapter 9

Lydia

This is the best Star Rangers gig ever. They are such a great party band. Molly, Kate, and I are dancing at the front, howling along to the songs we know and love, waving our hands in the air, having a wonderful time.

I can't believe that Sheena missed tonight. I set up the perfect opportunity for her to hang out with lovely Luke and she's not even here. But then, I glance over, through the crowd of heads and waving hands, and there's Sheena with Cam and Luke. She must have only just arrived.

I nudge Kate and elbow Molly then use my thumb, in a disco dance move, to point in the direction of Luke and Sheena who appear to be in deep conversation. Both my friends give me a double thumbs up and I pat myself on the back. Finally, Sheena has seen sense. Now I can enjoy the night and party with my gal pals.

The next tune on the Star Rangers set list is one of my all-time favorites, the Guns 'N' Roses hit, 'Sweet Child of Mine'. The noise around us is deafening as everyone sings along with this crowd-pleasing hit. I'm enthralled in the middle of the dance floor until I nosily sneak a peek to see how Sheena and Luke are getting along. My vision is obscured somewhat by a bunch of fellow revelers. I squint in the colored stage lights between arms, heads, and torsos to glimpse the three people watching from the side wall by the door. But there are only two. Sheena isn't there any-more. I figure she must be at the bar or in the bathroom, so I keep dancing and singing loudly, "Oh, oh, oh, sweet child of mine!"

Dylan plays a fantastic guitar solo, followed by a re-sounding blast from the drummer before the bass player has his time to shine. Olly, the vocalist, sings the final elongated vowels of the last chorus then the song winds up with a huge bashy ending, with all players hammering out the last chord as if their lives depend on it. The band members seem happy with their show. There are smiles all round. They bow and wave to the crowd as if they are in a massive stadium rather than a small-town bar.

Olly waits for the applause to die down, then he says, "We're going to slow things down a little now, ladies and gentlemen, with a Bon Jovi hit I'm sure you all know. Don't be shy. If there's someone you've had your eye on tonight, go ahead. Make your move. This is 'Always'." Dylan plays the familiar intro then he's joined by the bass player and the drummer. People around me join together in pairs, enjoying the shared moment of dancing close. Cam appears and takes Molly's hand. He wraps his arms around her, and they begin to sway in time.

Feeling a bit awkward, I smile at Kate, and she leads me back to the bar. I check for Luke and Sheena. Perhaps they're slow dancing or have gone somewhere quieter to talk; exchange numbers; arrange a date; plan the rest of their lives together. I sniff back a sob as the emotion of this idea fills me with happiness. But also, a strange sense of loss that I can't account for. However, when Kate and I get back to our spot by the wall, I only see Luke. Sheena isn't there.

Unfazed I ask Luke over the noise, "Are you having a good time?"

"Yes. Thank you," Luke bends down to my ear. The music for 'Always' isn't as loud as it was for the rockier numbers, and I can hear what he's saying.

I look around. "Where's Sheena?"

"She left. She said she had a migraine coming on."

"Oh no." I'm so sad. And also annoyed that my plan had not played out as I had hoped.

"Not the best environment for a headache," says Luke leaning close, so close I inhale his scent, a mix of fresh air and warm earth. I am inches from his chest and part of me wants to sink my face into his blue chambray shirt. I check myself and stop just in time.

"That's too bad. And they played this song," I say out loud without expanding on the significance.

"It's funny how certain songs affect you. I mean, I remember hearing this for the first time. And wow. I loved it." Luke smiles at me. "Lydia, would you like to dance?"

Now I'm conflicted. The perfect romantic song is being played and the most beautiful man in the room has asked me to dance. My heart flutters but a tug in my brain says, *Stop! He's taken. You set him up with Sheena. He's not for you, dumbass.* Then another part of my brain is saying, *Sheena isn't here anymore. The handsome man is asking... you. You lucky, lucky girl! Woohoo!*

It's a dance. It's nothing more than that. It's a friend dance. We can be friends and still slow dance to this tune without any romantic implications. Of course, we can.

Luke takes my hand and leads me to the edge of the dance floor where the lights have dimmed. I could just not dance. Say thanks but no thanks. I should walk away in the opposite direction. Make an excuse. *I need to powder my nose. I've chipped a nail. I've just remembered, I've left the iron on.*

Luke stands in front of me and gently takes my hands in his. Couples hold each other and sway with the pulse of the song. Then Luke's hands drop to my waist, and I feel the warmth of his body close to mine. I sense his chest inside the light cotton shirt and the proximity of him creates a whoosh of blood surging in my veins. My heart beats fast. Light-headed and dizzy from dancing, something inside me wants to run a mile from this man. The sensation is too intense. I'm feeling unnerved by his closeness. And yet, something else wants to stay slow dancing with Luke Maddox forever.

Stop being so dramatic, I tell myself. It's just dancing. But Luke is so very near, and the man in him is saying things to the woman in me, without my consent. Painfully aware that the song is going on and on, I become stiff with anxiety. Self-conscious. Awkward. I want to break away from Luke, jump on the stage, and pull the plug on the band's sound system.

I feel sick. This wasn't what I had planned. Sheena was supposed to be in my place. She's the one wanting a boyfriend, not me. This is all wrong. And yet. Luke smells amazing. Something earthy, like wild thyme, but fresh like parsley or sage. His scent overwhelms the thinking, rational part of my brain. I want to reach my arms around his neck and pull his mouth to mine and kiss him within an inch of his life.

Finally, thankfully, the music stops before I totally embarrass myself. The couples surrounding us all seem to be caught up in a heartfelt embrace, a beautiful romantic moment they are sure to treasure well into old age. Cam strokes Molly's hair and whispers something into her ear which makes her wrap her arms around his torso and pull her husband closer still. They entwine their fingers and stand blissfully motionless.

Feeling trapped, I push Luke away, shake his hand as if he's a bank manager, and say, "Thanks for the dance." I nod politely. "It was nice." I sound like a robot; something mechanical; the Tin Man in the Wizard of Oz.

"Yes. It was." He smiles and puts his hands in the pockets of his jeans. "And thank you, Lydia."

We stand facing each other as I calculate how fast I could run to the exit. I'm breathing heavily. Luke is still so close. Someone bumps into him from behind causing him to step forward and against me.

"Excuse me," he says protectively taking me into his arms again, briefly, before releasing me. "It's crowded, isn't it? Do you want to go back to the bar? Or maybe we could take a walk somewhere quiet."

Take a walk somewhere quiet? That is what was supposed to happen with Sheena, not me.

"Thanks for coming out tonight, Oak River," Olly says into the mike which breaks the intimacy of the loved-up couples. "This is our last number. We love you. Be safe. Good night. See you again soon."

Chapter 10

Luke

Holding Lydia, as we danced, was the highlight of my night; my week; my year. She fits inside the circle of my arms as if she is meant to be there. Her hair smells incredible. I want to bury my nose in the silky tresses that fall around her shoulders. We sway together in time to the music, and it feels like heaven. The crowd melts away, and it's as if Lydia and I are the only people in the place. The band is playing this song just for us, 'Always'. And yet we hardly know each other. All I know is, I feel I'm home.

Abruptly, Lydia pulls away from me, breaking the beautiful, intimate, slow-dance spell. She holds out her hand for a formal handshake and says, "Thanks for the dance. It was nice."

It was nice? Is that what she really thinks? It was more than nice for me. It was wonderful. I want to ask her what happened. But then, it was just a dance. And how I felt could have been my imagination running wild. It's been a while since I held a pretty woman. The experience must have gotten to me, and I projected deeper feelings of something more than just a dance.

The frontman announces the last song of the night. The music changes and I follow Lydia back to the bar. I figure it's time to go. I stand close to Lydia with my eye on the exit. There's so much I'd like to say, but the music is too loud. There are too many people. I look down at the floor. My hands are stuck in the pockets of my jeans.

"Thanks for inviting me." I lean in to kiss Lydia's cheek. "I had a great time tonight."

"Me too," says Lydia. Friendly but cautiously distant.

Whatever I felt when we were slow dancing together is obviously a mistake. Lydia has made it crystal clear that there's no way she's interested in me, romantically. Which is fine. I like her. Maybe we can see each other again, socially. As a friend. A buddy. A pal. Or whatever. I don't know. At least I do know where I stand. The final chords of the last song ring out.

"Well, goodnight, Lydia."

"Goodnight, Luke."

ele

Monday and the start of a new week. I'm in the main barn with Ray, Amy, Georgia, Saskia, and the part-time staff who have taken up positions, seated on hay bales around me. They each hold a printout of the run sheet and assigned duties for the upcoming Open Day. We talk through what the day might deliver and cover any questions and concerns that arise. My laptop is open and I'm referring to the detailed documents created by Maisy - a color-coded calendar; staff roster; health and safety procedures; and clear instructions for every aspect of the Green Acres Grand Open Day.

"The day is mainly for local people to come and have a look around; for us to introduce ourselves; and to showcase what we're all about." My staff listen attentively. "We're a stud farm first, but the Open Day is for trialing our new venture in horseback rides, treks, and riding lessons. Pretty much, if someone would like to ride a horse, then we can accommodate. Hopefully, our visitors will like what they see, book a trek or riding lessons, tell their friends, and come back again and again."

There are still things to sort out, but mostly everything's in place. Maisy ordered more riding gear so we can take up to six people trekking at one time. The ponies we have are suitable for beginners. And the staff now all have the relevant certification for leading a group and instructing.

"As you know, bookings come through the website, as well as over the phone, so it's super important you are all familiar with the program. If you're not sure about anything, or it's a special request, then grab the name and number and say that someone will get back in touch very soon." I pause for a minute and look around at the faces who smile back at me. I'm encouraged by their willingness and positive outlook. "This is new for me too, so we're all learning." My staff nod an affirmative. "Having visitors onsite, it kind of means that we're 'on show', if that makes sense. So, be friendly but courteous. Helpful. And be prepared to answer questions about the horses and stables. We're going to get reps from the hotel in town, and other tourist-related businesses. So, this is a great way to connect with the community, show off what we're all about. We'll get families. There will be kids, so be extra careful to keep everyone safe." I ask if there are any questions, then wait, and look around the barn. Everyone seems happy. "The weather looks good which is great for the outdoor demo. The whole thing, including the prize giveaway, should be all wrapped up in a couple of hours, tops."

"It's going to be great," says Saskia. "Maisy's flyers look really good."

"They're up in the library and noticeboards around town," says Georgia.

"I've invited some industry people and we're getting some RSVPs through," I say looking at my email inbox. "The final head count should be this Thursday. Of course, everyone is welcome, but we need them to register so we know how many people are on site." Everyone nods and smiles. "Brilliant. Thank you. That's all for today."

I close my laptop, and the staff members stand, stretch, and chat quietly together before heading out to their various stableyard duties. Walking back to the house, I shout hello to Deedee who is enjoying the paddock. He prances around, with his tail held high, showing off to the ladies in the paddock next door. He's a fine animal. I'd really love to go for a ride right now, but I have a ton of admin and accounts to do.

In the office, I plug in my laptop, sit down, and try to concentrate on accounts, income, and expenses. But my mind is distracted by the memory of dancing with Lydia a couple of weeks before. I can still feel her in my arms and the way we moved to the slow song.

It's been a while since I felt I could hold a woman that wasn't Courtney. I respectfully held back from Lydia. And Lydia? She didn't need to tell me in words that she's not interested in me. The handshake spoke volumes. I lean back in my chair, interlacing my fingers together behind my head, and gaze out of the window.

It's better for us to be just friends. This is a small town, after all. I know how things work. Just because you dance with a lady, some folk could see that as the start of something. Something that leads to something else. I need to protect myself. I don't want to be the subject of gossip. And I don't want complications. Or heartbreak, if things go wrong. I've learned my lesson the hard way. I can't open my heart to someone for fear of it being trashed. Like before. With Courtney.

Memories of Courtney instantly chill my bones. My heart hardens. My jaw clenches. Falling in love is never going to happen to me again.

Chapter 11

Lydia

After the epic fail at the Star Rangers gig. I'm hard-pressed to come up with another idea for my Luke/Sheena pairing. Perhaps I should let them steer their own love ship and trust that they'll get together without my help. But someone needs to take that first step. Sheena is pretending to be cool, and Luke just seems too shy. Anyway, my matchmaking has been pushed to the back burner because of Rita and Brodie's wedding preparations and some new bookings that I need to follow up.

In the workshop at Blossoms in Bloom, I assemble a mood board for a silver wedding anniversary. The couple's family is throwing a surprise party at the church hall here in Oak River. It's a sizable space to transform into a party fit for a silver celebration. But I've done it before a number of times. The church hall is a blank canvas for me to design with color, form, and fragrance.

According to my notes from the consultation, they want loads of blue hues and lavender. The centerpiece is all worked out. It will be a massive wicker heart that I already have in my props store. It gets reused a lot for various events and occasions. The woven wicker is ideal for threading flowers, leaves, trails of vines, ribbons, and twinkly fairy lights. When the heart structure is festooned with blooms it guarantees a 'wow' factor when guests arrive at a venue.

I hear the bells tinkle as someone comes into the store. Marty says hi. It's someone we know. I half listen to what Marty is saying, then he taps the door to my workshop.

"Hi, Lydia." Molly pokes her head in. "I hope I'm not interrupting."

"Hey," I say looking up from the laptop screen and removing my glasses. "Not at all. What's up?"

"Have you seen this?" Molly waves a folded piece of glossy green paper at me. A flyer, some advertising material, I'm guessing. She walks toward me then lays the brochure down on my worktable. Clear white letters read Green Acres – Horseback Riding & Treks. "Someone dropped off a stack of these at the library this morning."

"How cool," I say picking up the brochure and turning it over to read more. "I can't remember the last time I went on a horse. Must have been at least ten years ago."

Molly smiles and her eyes twinkle. "That's not all. There's an Open Day at the ranch this Saturday and it's free to go. You just need to register online."

"Wow." My mind flips into hyper-drive as I piece Luke and Sheena together, like a jigsaw, in various romantic situations: sunset on horseback; hand in hand on the trail; picnic at a gorgeous viewpoint; relaxing on the porch with a glass of vintage Merlot. Love. Smiles. A Happy Ever After. "Let's register right now." I hurriedly type the web address into the browser.

"Okay. I'd love to go. Cam is working, so he can't make it."

"So, you, me, and Sheena. That would be good." I click on the registration page and scroll down.

"Alright. I didn't think about Sheena," says Molly. "But yeah. Why not?"

"Well, things didn't really go according to plan at the Star Rangers gig. She had a migraine, left early, and missed the opportunity to slow dance with Luke."

"Lydia! I thought we'd talked about that, and we agreed to leave love to take its natural course... *What will be, will be.*"

"No. That's not what I remember." I find the website and click the button to register for the event. "Anyway, for whatever reason, it didn't work out for them at the gig. So, I think the Open Day gives them another go. Another bite of the cherry, so to speak. Don't you think?"

"Well, from where I was standing, it looked very much as if all the romance was happening to you, my friend."

"When?"

"At the gig. When they played that Bon Jovi song," Molly says enunciating each syllable as if I'm hard of hearing.

"No. I don't think so. I mean, yes, it's true, I danced with Luke. And I don't know what you think you saw, Molly. But it was like dancing with my grandpa." I turn my attention to my phone and pretend to be busy.

"Whatever." Molly gives me one of her looks, then wanders around my workroom looking at the semi-chaos of half-finished bouquets and arrangements; color charts; botanical posters; shelves of vases; buckets and other receptacles. "Don't you think you should call Sheena to find out if she's free to come?"

"Ah, yes. You're right." I hadn't considered that Sheena wouldn't be free to finally connect with her handsome cowboy at his ranch.

I dial Sheena's number. She picks up straight away. "Lydia! I was just about to call you."

"You were?"

"There's an Open Day at the Dixon place," Sheena says enthusiastically.

"Green Acres – Horseback Riding & Treks?"

"That's right. I still think of it as the Dixon place," says Sheena laughing. "I'll need to practice saying Green Acres if I'm going to be recommending horseback rides to our guests. Anyway, the reason I wanted to call you is, I get to go as part of a work thingy. And because I am the senior customer relations manager, I get first dibs and get paid to play. But, of course, it's important for staff to know what activities to offer our guests. So, I was wondering if you'd like to come with me?"

"Yes. That would be awesome." I grin and wave at Molly. "In fact, Molly is here now showing me the flyer. It looks like fun. I'm on the Open Day registration page on the website right now." I scan the information on my screen.

"We get shown around the stables. There's a horse training demo."

"And, it says here, there's a cool prize draw that'll be announced on the day," says Sheena excitedly.

"Great."

Before Sheena hangs up the call, she says that she's taking the hotel car, because it's a work thingy, but there'll be space for Molly and me, if we want to join her and get a ride over.

I'm excited. This couldn't be more perfect. This is the event that seals the matchmaking deal. There's nothing like being outside in the fresh air for getting to know someone. And once Sheena sees Luke in his element, on a horse at the ranch, there's no way her heart won't melt to mush. And when Luke sees how much Sheena fits into his outdoors, cowboy life, he will fall head over heels. No doubt about that. My matchmaking work here is done (almost). I squeal on the inside.

———*ele*———

Saturday arrives. At Blossoms in Bloom, I finalize the design and quotes for the silver wedding and email the documents to the client.

It's helpful to offer tiered budget options for any event: Basic, includes the centerpiece and one table arrangement; Deluxe, includes the centerpiece, table arrangements, and two stands; and Wowzers, includes the centerpiece, table arrangements, five stands, plus garlands and fairy lights on walls and ceiling, and anything else the client has on their wish list. In my experience, a client will consider the Basic first, then nearly always opt for Wowzers in the end.

"It should be pretty quiet today," I say to Marty as I lean on the counter watching for Sheena's car. "I think we're on top of everything regarding the wedding. If you could do a window, that would be brilliant."

"Great. No problem," says Marty tidying the rolls of ribbon. "Do you have a theme in mind or are you going to leave it completely up to me?"

"Marty. I trust you one hundred percent. Do one of your showstoppers."

"Fab."

Sheena pulls up outside Blossoms in Bloom and toots for me. I grab my purse and wave to Marty as I shoot out of the store.

"I feel like I'm skipping school," I say as I climb into the back seat of the hotel car. Molly sits up front, beside Sheena. "This is going to be fun."

"Yes. Fun and I'm getting paid...," says Sheena. She shifts the car into gear and pulls away from the curb. "...which is a bonus because my new kitchen is going to be fantastic. Although, it's not cheap. Everything is top of the range, state of the art."

"I can't wait to see it, when it's all done," I say, leaning forward to listen to Sheena.

"And I can't wait to have you over for a marvelous dinner that I'm going to cook. Oh my. I'm so happy with what Gary's doing. He's completely ripped out the horrible old units that I've hated for years. Since Archie walked out." Sheena indicates then turns down the street leading out of town. "I tell you, getting your living space worked on is like therapy. It really is."

"That's so good to hear, Sheena," says Molly.

"I was going to say you have more pep in your step these days." I dig Molly's ribs without Sheena noticing. "Is it just a new kitchen, or is there something else going on?"

"Oh, I think it's the kitchen. And I feel good. Really good."

"It's a shame you left the Star Rangers gig early," says Molly. "They played one of my all-time favorite Bon Jovi songs, 'Always'."

"I love that song," says Sheena dreamily. "I remember slow dancing with Archie to that song at a high-school dance. We were very young."

"Well, you could have slow danced with Luke to that song. It's a shame you had a migraine and had to go home."

"Oh yeah. It was a shame. The music was way too loud for me. Migraines are no fun, at all." Sheena drives to the highway. "Did you have a good night?"

"Yes, we did," I say thinking about slow dancing with Luke. "I had the best dance... with Kate and Molly. But we missed you."

A stab of guilt causes me to wince. I twist uncomfortably in the back seat. I did miss Sheena on Friday. I had the date all set up for her to dance with Luke. Then when she left and Luke danced with me, that turned things around. But only a bit.

I'm going to do my best to follow through with matchmaking a friend who needs me to do just that. I can't be falling for the target. That would be ridiculous, against my better judgment and the rules of matchmaking. Although memories of the slow dance and the words of Bon Jovi's 'Always', fill up my imagination and turn me all gooey on the inside.

Chapter 12

Luke

I check my watch. The Open Day guests will be arriving soon. My team has been amazing. The stableyard is spotless - spick and span. I'm impressed by how everyone is on task. There's a real sense of pride today. But I still have pre-event jitters. I walk around to calm myself. I'm a little nervous about having the townsfolk in my backyard, and I hope I'm not showing it.

Down at the gate, Amy is stationed in her high-viz jacket, sun hat, and shades, ready to direct visitors to the paddock we've roped off for parking. She waves, then smiles at me, and gives me a double thumbs up.

The new printed signage, tied along the fencing by the entrance, looks fantastic. Green Acres is clear and bold in white typeface, with the website and phone number printed under a photo of Deedee, majestically in full gallop. Maisy's design, of course. She called to get an update on how things were going; to make sure I wasn't messing things up. She's smarter than I give her credit for.

The afternoon is relatively informal. I'll make a short welcome speech in the barn. Then I'll invite everyone to take a tour around the stableyard and tack room and ask any questions they may have. After that, there's a training demonstration, where Ray will take Bernie, one of our yearlings, around the stable paddock on a lunge line. Ray's calm and good with the young horses. Then I'll ride out on Deedee and show the crowd what he can do. I've taught him some tricks. I hope he wants to work with me and doesn't decide to display his famous attitude where he just stubbornly stands still. But I don't think that there'll be a problem today. He loves showing off. He knows he's the star of the show. After the demo, I'll invite everyone back to the barn for refreshments and we'll do the prize draw.

I check my watch again. The weather has held out. It's a little chilly but not raining. I can see visitors' vehicles kick up dust as they slow to make the turn onto the ranch driveway. The parking lot paddock is filling up with rows of cars, vans, and trucks. I hear laughter and excited voices as families and groups of people follow the bright green arrows directing them through the stableyard and into the barn.

Amy radios to say the last carload is on their way. The main gate is closed. It's showtime. I take a wireless mike and climb onto a hay bale. Noisy chatter automatically dies down in anticipation. The expectant crowd turns their attention toward me. Suddenly I'm self-conscious, and I almost forget what I've been practicing. Thankfully, Maisy printed out what I need to say in large, easy-to-read bullet points. I unfold the sheet of paper that I tucked into my shirt pocket and take a minute to look around at the faces in the crowd. I spot Lydia near the back. She smiles and raises her hand. The sight of her pretty face and her warm smile calms my nerves and encourages me to continue.

"Hello everyone and welcome to Green Acres. Thanks for taking the time to come to our Open Day. My name is Luke Maddox of Maddox Holdings, my family's company. I'm Texan born and bred. Do we have any other Texans here?" I listen for a yay, but there's silence, so I keep going. "We've prepared some activities that I hope you'll enjoy, but mostly, this is an opportunity for us to get to know you, and for you to see what we're working on out here, horse-wise. Our main business is breeding. Horses, that is." Some people laugh. "But our new venture is horseback riding and trekking. We have a short program this afternoon. It's on the registration page on the website..." I hold up my phone. "... and you'll find it pinned up on the stable doors. If you have any questions, please don't hesitate to ask our staff members, Amy, Ray, Georgia, and Saskia." My staff members raise their hands as I say their names. "They're all wearing the fashionable high-viz orange vests. So, I hope you have a good time here today. After the demos, we'll meet back here for drinks and snacks, and we'll find out the winner of our grand prize. I'll hand the mike to Georgia, and she'll tell you about the horses we have here on the ranch and why the American Quarter Horse is the best breed in the world."

Georgia hops on the hay bale beside me and takes the microphone. She's like a game show host, the way she works the crowd, unlike me who is not at all comfortable in the spotlight. As the visitors show their appreciation for Georgia's informative and entertaining insights, Ray leaves to get organized in the training paddock.

"If there are no further questions, then please follow me to the training demonstration," Georgia says with a big smile. She hops down from the hay bale and leads the crowd, Pied Piper-like, outside.

Some folks in the crowd stop me to shake my hand and introduce themselves. I should be paying more attention, but I'm distracted by Lydia. She's happily talking with a knot of people. I'm drawn to her and make my way over to where she is.

"Howdy. It's nice to see some familiar faces," I say making a point of addressing the group and not just Lydia. "Thanks for coming all the way out here today."

"Well, thank you, Mr Maddox...," says Sheena beaming.

"Luke," I interrupt. "No need for formalities. Besides, Mr Maddox is my dad."

"Luke." Sheena smiles, then says, "Trekking and horseback rides will be a huge draw card to the area. I've added the flyers to the Welcome folders in each room. Some people say that there's very little to do in Oak River, but I believe we have a lot to offer visitors."

"I think so too," says Molly. "I love to showcase our community at the library. We have a wonderful library, Luke. You must call in sometime soon to set up your membership."

"I will. Thank you. I like to read."

"Yes well, we have an extensive selection of titles. And if you have a request for something specific, I can track it down for you." Molly smiles warmly. "We often borrow books from the central library in Richmond."

"If you like hiking, we have a wonderful national park close by," says Lydia. "In fact, one of the gates is just at the top of this road. And Dylan, the guitarist in Star Rangers, is a trail guide and runs camping trips."

"That's right. He does," says Molly brightly. "Their last gig was so, so good, wasn't it? I love that they added the Bon Jovi song."

The mention of 'Always' sends a jolt sparking through me. I can almost feel the touch of Lydia in my arms again as we slow-danced to the love song. I avoid her gaze, fearful that my expression will betray my emotions.

"And let's not forget about the Annual Spring Fair. I think I've already told Luke about it," says Sheena snapping me out of my reverie. "That's what Oak River is most famous for. Everyone wants to see the War of Independence battle re-enactment. It's so exciting. I see it every year and it always gives me goosebumps. You know, the Historical Society is always advertising for new members. Could you see yourself as a rebel, Luke. Or would you wave the British colors and be a baddie for the day?"

"I think I'd have to be a rebel." I sneak a quick glance at Lydia who holds my gaze for a moment.

"Oh yes," says Sheena brightly. "I can just imagine you riding at the head of the charge, bearing the flag of independence. How thrilling would that be?" I feel suddenly shy, but thankfully Sheena continues, redirecting the focus of the conversation away from me. "Lydia organizes the Floral Design Competition. You'd be forgiven for believing that the battle re-enactment would be the epitome of contest. But no. Until you witness it for yourself, you have no idea that flower arranging could be so competitive. Talk about knives out."

I check the time. "Let's go and watch Ray in action. He's going to be training Bernie. He's still a young horse and can be a little feisty."

I lead the group out of the stableyard and up the track that leads to the paddock. The other visitors are evenly spread out along the fence to watch. Ray approaches Bernie calmly holding the halter loosely in his hands. He's showing it to the colt, so the animal gets familiar with it. The young horse is timid and shies away, trotting to the other side of the fenced area. Slowly, Ray walks toward him. When the horse looks like it's going to move. Ray stops until the colt is calm again. Then he walks steadily toward it again.

After a few minutes, the halter is on the horse's head with the lead attached. The crowd applauds politely. Ray strokes Bernie's neck. Then steps away leading the horse in a circle around the paddock.

"You can see how Ray is communicating with the animal. He's building trust with everything he's doing."

Ray lets out more length of the lead and encourages the horse to walk in a circle around him. Then Ray taps his whip on the horse's rump to get Bernie to trot. He's flighty and rears up, but Ray is persistent and, in a while, the young horse settles into an easy stride and moves with rhythmic grace.

"It takes a few sessions in the paddock like this, to train a horse for riding, the way we do it. You need patience and skill. But I've witnessed gauchos in Argentina break in wild stallions in a day. It's unbelievable how they do that."

Ray is almost done with Bernie's training session. I leave to get Deedee. He's saddled up and waiting for me in his stable. I lead him out and enter the paddock through the side gate, avoiding the spectators whose attention is still on Ray and Bernie.

Chapter 13

Lydia

Picturing Luke riding at the head of the rebels in the battle re-enactment causes an involuntary gasp and a quickening of pulse. The idea of him charging to victory, however re-enacted and theatrical, overwhelms me in an unexpected tingly way.

While we are watching Ray train Bernie, Luke leaves us. Then minutes later, I turn my head and out of the corner of my eye, I spot Luke walking Deedee up to a gate in the paddock fence on the other side, away from the audience. Ray leads Bernie out and holds the gate while Luke mounts his horse and rides into the training paddock. Deedee canters in a wide circle, his muscular neck is arched, his nostrils flared.

Watching Luke ride Deedee is astonishing. He's at one with the powerful stallion. Every movement is subtle and looks effortless. Deedee seems to enjoy showing off for the crowd. He tosses his long, flowing mane and swishes his tail as he prances with knees high. Luke makes him turn on the spot, walk backward, then run full gallop from one end of the training ring, kicking up dust, to the other. I could watch them all day. Then, Deedee walks sedately around in a circle before rearing up, like Champion the Wonder Horse. Luke dismounts and stands beside his horse and together they bow to the spectators, causing a gush of 'Ahhhs' from everyone, especially me, and a round of appreciative applause.

"Thank you, ladies and gentlemen," says Ray who is perched on the fencing rail. "I hope you enjoyed our demonstration. If you'd like to return to the barn, we're going to serve some light refreshments and, most importantly, we're going to do the prize draw." He hops down and walks to the barn followed by a trail of visitors.

"Wasn't that amazing?" says Molly with shining eyes. "Luke is a proper cowboy, just like in the movies, isn't he? I'm quite overwhelmed."

"Me too," I say quietly as if I've had a spiritual epiphany. Angels sing inside my head, and everything is shiny.

"He is a very good rider," Sheena says. "No doubt about that. But I wonder what health and safety procedures they have in place here. I'd like to know more before I send our guests here. The last thing I want is to feel that we're liable for an unsafe activity."

We join the other guests in the barn and accept a beaker of soda from the trays that are being circulated. Platters of baked savories and potato chips are set up on trestle tables around the barn's periphery. Containers with pens and pencils sit next to strips of paper that sit under small rocks, to stop them from blowing away.

The chatter surrounding me is praise for a great show. I stand with my friends, but I keep an eye on the door and watch for Luke. In a few minutes, I see him. He takes off his hat, hands it to one of his staff, then steps onto the hay bale and waits for the chatter to die down.

"Okay, folks. That's about it for today. Thanks for coming out. We appreciate your interest in seeing what we're all about out here at Green Acres." Some people start clapping. He clears his throat. "So, all we need to do now is find a lucky winner for our prize draw of a voucher for a complimentary horse trek for two." There are some excited whoops from the crowd. "Alright then," says Luke smiling broadly. "You'll notice the writing equipment collated on the tables." We all turn to look around. "Without causing a riot. Let's allow the ladies to go first. All you have to do is write your name on a piece of paper then fold it and put it into one of our hats. Then, gentlemen, it'll be your turn."

There's a scurry of activity as women swoop down onto the pens and pencils, making a flurry of bits of paper. The mayhem lasts a few seconds, and I wait for it to die down before I approach the closest table. I reach for a pencil and a handful of paper, then very quickly I scribble a name, and then another and another. In the blink of an eye, I stuff my handful of paper into a waiting hat. Then I stand back as the male contingent begins writing their names and tossing them into the hats too.

Luke, who is still standing on the hay bale, takes back his hat and adds the contents of four more hats. Then he theatrically rummages around in the loose slips of paper. "Drum roll please." Ray and the other staff members lean forward and rapidly pat their thighs creating a drumroll simulation. Luke pulls out a piece of paper, unfolds it, and holds it up. He clears his throat then says, "And the winner is Sheena D." Luke searches the crowd.

"Oh my," says Sheena. Her hands snap up to her chest in surprise. "It's me. I've won."

"Where's Sheena?" says Luke shielding his eyes as he looks for her. One of his staff members hands him a printed piece of paper. "Come on up here." Sheena squeals gleefully and totters through the excited crowd to accept her prize. "Congratulations, Sheena. This voucher entitles you and a friend to a half-day horse trek here at Green Acres."

Sheena beams and she looks emotional, as if she's going to cry. Then she says thank you a few times, while the crowd claps and cheers, before hurrying back to where we're waiting.

"This is so great," she says grinning. "I don't think I've won anything in my whole life."

"Congratulations!" Molly and I say together.

As the barn empties out, I watch for Luke. He's chatting with people and shaking their hands. I can see that he's busy, so we wave goodbye. Then, to my surprise, he smiles and comes over.

"Thanks for coming, ladies. I hope you had a good time. And, congratulations, Sheena. Just call to book your trek. We'll try and accommodate any day you want, except Christmas, of course."

"Alright, thanks so much," says Sheena still buzzing from her win. "I'll let you know."

Luke smiles. He looks as if he's going to say something more, but he just nods. "See you soon, then." His glance catches my eye for a moment before he turns and strides away and I'm left feeling a bit woozy.

I wonder if he has counted all the 'Sheena' entries. Will he revoke her prize if he suspects cheating? Or will he think Sheena's multiple entries are endearing and an indication of her excited enthusiasm? Of course, my plan may still backfire depending on Luke's perception of contest fixing. It's probably best if he doesn't check the names in the hat. I cross my fingers and hope. But I figure, if Luke was going to say anything about it, he would have done so by now.

A small, satisfied sigh escapes my lips. Is my work here done? Perhaps. But then, I can't help admiring Luke's tall, strong frame and the easy glide to his walk. Yay. Go Sheena. There's no better way to get to know someone than being out and about, riding the range on horseback. Although... What is that niggly feeling? Jealousy? Nah. It can't be. It's probably indigestion from the snacks and soda, and the thrill of being in the crowd of spectators watching an awesome show. Or the effects of cheating on behalf of my single friend.

Two days before Rita and Brodie's wedding, I call Luke to say I'm coming to get some crabapple branches from his trees.

"Yes. Of course, I'll be here." I melt a little listening to Luke's voice on the phone. "Just turn up. Do you need anything? Hacksaw, perhaps?"

"No. Thanks. I've done this a million times." I try and act cool. "I have everything I need, and a helper, so... Thanks again for letting me prune your trees."

"Anytime."

I'm hoping I don't see Luke as I drive out to Green Acres. The way I feel about him isn't supposed to be happening. It's not in the grand plan for me to fall for my friend's potential boyfriend that I have organized. Laura is with me in the van. I figured this was a two-person job and also, I don't want the opportunity of being alone with Luke just in case I give in to my feelings. The quicker we get the branches to the venue the better the result.

I drive in through the main gate and park close to the crabapple trees. I cut the engine and get out. Then I look up the hill at the horses in the paddock with the trees behind. It's peaceful and so beautiful.

"Right then, I guess we'll take a couple of branches from each tree, so they won't look too damaged and the tree won't suffer." Laura takes the tarpaulin from the back of the van while I grab the tools. "Look for branches with the most fruit."

Laura lays a tarp on the ground, and we get to work sawing what we need from the trees. The apples are so beautiful. Perfectly round and the colors of autumn - golds, reds, oranges. They are going to look amazing as the centerpiece in the marquee. We need to be really careful not to bruise the apples, otherwise they'll turn brown and rotten in no time.

Using crabapple branches is an experiment, kind of. I haven't used them much before in previous designs because, even though the fruit stays looking good, the leaves tend to curl and dry out in a matter of hours. So, I've made up a solution of glycerine, benzoic acid, sulphates, and potassium sorbates that I plan to spray onto the branches to preserve the color and stop the leaves from curling. It won't stop the eventual decay, but it'll be enough for the event. Still, I have my fingers crossed that my homemade preservative will work. Sometimes I feel like a mad professor in my lab testing formulas and mixing ratios of this and that.

I hear a car engine as I hack away at a particularly attractive branch. I peek out through the leaves and see that it's Luke driving. I squirm and hide as best as I can in between the branches of the tree, hoping he won't see me and continue on his way. But no. He pulls over and winds down his window.

"Hey, Lydia. Are you getting what you need?" he asks in his caramelly southern accent.

It's clear that my camouflage isn't working, so I step out from the tree holding a branch as if it has special powers to deflect Luke's animal magnetism. It doesn't. It's just a crabapple branch. And I am just a woman covered in leaves and dust, wanting to be invisible.

We exchange some pleasantries, then I say, "We had a wonderful time at the Open Day. You were amazing on Deedee... I mean, you and Ray put on a great show."

"Thanks. I'm happy you came."

"Yes. We all had a great time. Especially Sheena. She loved it."

"And she won the prize draw too."

"That's right," I say awkwardly. "So, has she been in touch to book a ride, yet?"

"I don't think so."

"Well, she will. And soon, I expect. She told me that she couldn't wait to get in the saddle with you. I mean... on a horseback ride."

Laura appears from behind a tree close by. She's carrying a handsaw and a branch loaded with little apples. I introduce her to Luke. Laura smiles and says hi, then carefully lays the branch down on the tarp cloth, and disappears behind another tree.

"These apples are so pretty," I say deflecting my attention away from the handsome cowboy in the truck.

"Yes. You're right. I hadn't considered the humble crabapple as decoration before, but I can see what you mean." Luke smiles his devastating smile, and I wish that he would move along so I can stop feeling wobbly and get back to what I'm supposed to be doing. "So, Lydia." I love the way he says my name. "If I don't see you before I go, have a great Thanksgiving and Christmas."

"Ah, you too. Are you going back to your family for the holidays?"

"Eventually. I have some prospective clients to see. They have a breeding mare that I may be interested in. I want to see their setup in person. I don't trust pictures on the web."

"No. Me neither." Then I remember that Sheena is supposed to be trekking with Luke into the sunset. "So, when are you traveling? Soon?"

"Yeah. Next week. But Ray is here, and I have a great team to take care of things while I'm away."

"Great. That's great." But it doesn't give me much time.

Luke touches the brim of his hat then says, "I'll see you later, Lydia. I hope the crabapples work out for the wedding."

For a minute I forget that I'm holding a branch. I've squeezed it to my chest and crumpled the leaves. Luke shifts into gear and steers the truck down to the gate. I watch him go then lay the crabapple branch gently with the others, although I fear I may have bruised this one beyond repair. A moment later, Laura's head pops out between apple trees, and she waves to me.

"I think we have enough now," I yell straightening up and stretching my back. "Let's go."

Chapter 14

Luke

Lydia intrigues me. Sometimes when I see her, I think she likes me. She's friendly, open, and approachable. She looks directly into my eyes and it's as if she can see right through to my core, my soul. I'm hypnotized by her, and I can't turn away. But the very next time that we see each other, she is completely different. Her walls are up, and she doesn't meet my gaze. She's pushing me away and I get the impression that she isn't at all interested in knowing me on any level. And yet, I feel that there's something there. I felt the spark when we were slow-dancing. At least, I think I did. I'd like to clear my head of thoughts of Lydia, but she's in my mind when I wake up and I see her smile before I go to sleep. Am I being obsessive? Reading too much into things? I wish I knew more about her. It's like we're playing cat and mouse. But I don't want to play games.

At the ranch Open Day, she was so attentive and fun. I thought that, if there weren't so many people around, I'd ask her if she wanted to have dinner or something. Just the two of us. A couple of times when I looked for her in the crowd, she caught my eye and smiled right back. It sent a bolt of energy rushing through me that took my breath away. It was as if we were the only two people in the whole world. Nothing else mattered. When Lydia smiles, I feel connected. Warm on the inside. Home. Safe. I want to be close to her. When Lydia smiles, well, I just want more.

So, when she called to say she was coming over to cut some crabapple branches, I made sure I was around. I casually stopped by in my truck, as if I was on my way out.

A tarp cloth is spread out on the ground and Lydia is sawing off a branch close to the trunk at head height. She's wearing work clothes - jeans, a cotton shirt, and rubber boots. She's wearing safety goggles and protective gloves. Her hair is tied back in a scruffy ponytail which I find adorable. She expertly saws through the wood. Her friend holds the branch ready to take its weight. They exchange words and smiles as the branches are gently placed with others on the ground cloth. They seem pleased with their harvest as I slow the truck to a stop and wind down the window.

"Hey, do you need a hand?" I say leaning my elbow out of the window. My other hand is on the steering wheel. The engine idles in neutral.

"Hey, no thank you. We've got this." Lydia says smiling. She lifts her goggles onto the top of her head, but she doesn't make eye contact. "In fact, we're almost done." She introduces her friend. She looks at the ground, then someplace middle distance, but not at me. Then she lays another branch carefully on the tarp. Lydia is reserved and distant, so I shift the truck into gear and prepare to roll away, down the hill, to the gate.

Before I go, I open my mouth to ask about the prize draw and why she didn't enter. It's something that's been puzzling me. After I'd announced the winner, when everyone had gone home, I checked the pieces of paper with names written on. I couldn't find one from Lydia. It might have been lost or blown away, but Lydia was conspicuous by her absence. Did she really not want to enter? There were six pieces with Sheena's name. And here's what I find strange. Five of the six entries are just the name and an initial, written with blue pencil, in a kind of curly script, and one is the complete name, written in black ink using block capitals. Either Sheena must have really wanted to win and wrote her name multiple times to increase her chances. Or, and stranger still, someone else really wanted Sheena to win. I'm curious, but then it's not worth mentioning. I drew a winner and that's all that matters. So, I change my mind about saying anything about Sheena's multiple entries and tell Lydia that I'm going away.

"I'll be gone for the holidays," I say without revealing my emotions. Although my gut twists as I say the words. "I'm leaving next week."

Lydia stops what she's doing and stares at me looking confused, then she appears to be concerned, alarmed almost. "Oh, really? That's so soon," she says. Her eyes are wide. Does she want me to stay? Her expression is difficult to decipher.

I tell her that I have some clients to visit but then I'll have Thanksgiving with my family. Then I say, "I hope the crabapples work out for the wedding."

I wanted to say more but her friend appeared from the other side of a tree, so I thought better of it. As I drive away, I feel like a prize idiot, so I stop again at the gate. I'm about to throw the truck into reverse, back up, and ask Lydia out. But then, there's little point because I'm leaving soon.

I focus on the road ahead and keep driving but Lydia is on my mind. She's a conundrum, alright. Today she was polite and courteous, and I didn't feel anything more from her. Perhaps being friends is all I can expect or hope for. Do I want anything more? I keep thinking about it, so I guess the answer is, yes. I do want something more.

When I get back from the holidays, that'll be the time to take the step. I'll ask her out and we'll get to know each other and see how things go. I mean, I can't stop thinking about her. She's reeling me in, hook, line, and sinker. I need to give it my best shot and find out if there's anything more than friendship between us. Or maybe I'll just have to be content with the tragic truth, that you always want what you can't get. I'm sure there's a sad country song about that.

ele

Later, when I get home again, Maisy calls. She says she likes the photos I sent her, and she wants to find out how the Open Day went.

"It went well, thank you." I pace a track up and down the lounge carpet and look out at my newly pruned crabapple trees. I smile to myself. I didn't even know I had crabapples until a pretty lady showed up and told me.

"You mean it went off without a hitch?" Maisy asks, needling in her teasing way. "No one died?"

"You sound disappointed."

"Maybe. A little." She laughs. "So, you followed my instructions, and everything turned out perfect like I knew it would." Maisy gloats.

"Ah, yes. Well, I suppose the only teensy thing that was a bit chaotic was the prize draw. When we asked the guests to write their names on pieces of paper and put them in the hat."

"Okay. And you got them to do that first, before leaving the barn to watch the horse demos?"

"No. Afterwards. Because I forgot."

Maisy is laughing. "For heaven's sake. I leave you alone for five minutes and there's mayhem."

"It turned out okay. Nobody died. And we had a winner who was extremely excited to win." I didn't tell Maisy about Sheena's cheating tactic.

"Next time, huh?"

"Yes, ma'am." I deflect Maisy's attention away from my organizational shortfalls and tell her that everyone enjoyed the demonstration. "And we got our first bookings, so the event has already paid for itself. I'm happy."

"I'm so glad. I wish I was there." The line is quiet because I know she wants me to say, "I wish you were here too," but that's not true. I'm glad that Maisy is far away.

So, instead, I say, "It was great, Maisy. I have some more photos for you. I'll email them to you today, if you want?"

"That would be good. Thanks. I'll update your IG and FB." There's a pause in conversation then Maisy says, "So, I guess I'll see you at Thanksgiving?"

"Sure will."

I'm looking forward to some family time. My mom goes all out at Thanksgiving and Christmas. She has no off switch when it comes to festive food. I swear we eat leftovers well into the new year. My mom loves having us all together. I think she believes we wouldn't come and see her and Dad unless there is a mountain of our favorite treats that she remembers from when we were kids. Every year I tell her that she's gone too far. And every year she tells me not to be a Scrooge about it.

"Hey, Luke, when I see you, you can tell me all about how things are going with Crabapple Lady. You know, the pretty woman you met at the hotel?"

"What do mean, Maisy?" I say knowing full well what she means. But there's no way I'm going to open up to my meddling niece.

"Luke." She sighs down the line. "You're a red-blooded man with needs and wants..."

"Bye Maisy. Say hi to everyone and I'll see y'all soon." I hang up the phone in the nick of time. I don't need to be reminded that I'm a lonesome cowboy singing the blues.

Chapter 15

Lydia

The crabapples look even better than I anticipated. Their colors deepened beautifully, enriched by the dousing of my homemade preservative. Each apple has a wonderful dewy glow and the leaves have retained their freshness. With the help of Marty and Laura, I assemble as many of the structural arrangements in the workroom as I can and then load them into the Blossoms in Bloom van to transport them to the Carmichaels' homestead. We have the table arrangements; the wrought-iron stands that are to be placed on either side of the wedding party's table; the central display; and an abundance of extras, just in case. On the way out to the venue, I drop a few perfectly formed mini apples off at the café, for Kate to use on her cake. She is thrilled.

"They are gorgeous," Kate says clapping her hands like a child. "Do you have time for a coffee?" she asks as I head for the door, aware that time is ticking.

"Thanks, but no. I've got to dash. The sooner I get this lot up and in situ, the better I'll feel about the whole thing. It's going to take the best part of the morning, but I have a vision, and the effect will be stunning."

"No doubt, my friend. You're a creative genius." Kate blows me a kiss. "And I'll see you at the Carmichaels' soon with the cake," she says.

"I can't wait to see it. I'm sure it's absolutely perfect and it will make Rita cry. In the best way." I wave and then dart out to Marty who is waiting in the van with the engine running.

eee

With the wedding prep out of the way, and another set of happy clients, my next mission is to relax at my place with a glass of wine and a hot bath. I am pooped.

I took some photos of the wedding marquee before I left. And it did look amazing, even with the small army of caterers and techies swarming the place, getting everything ready for the guests who were due to arrive.

Kate brought the cake which was so beautiful it almost made me cry. She was dressed up and looking gorgeous too, as she was at the wedding as Rita's maid of honor. I hugged Kate and Dylan, Brodie's best man, and wished them a very happy day. I didn't see Rita, of course. She was still getting ready. Rita's mom and dad said that they loved what I had done, especially the apple element, which made me a bit emotional. So, Marty and I packed up as quickly as possible, and returned to Blossoms in Bloom, slightly ragged but content in the knowledge that we had done a fabulous job.

At home, after my frantic day, I remember my window of matchmaking opportunity is closing soon. Luke will be off for the holidays and Sheena will still be single. At Christmas. Not great, if you're feeling left on the shelf, as I suspect Sheena is. I need to act fast.

I dial Sheena's number. It rings. She picks up. I keep my voice upbeat but casual. "Hey, Sheena."

"Lydia."

I ignore the very curt greeting. She's probably had a rough day. "I was just wondering when you're going to book your pony trek."

"Oh, I don't know," Sheena sighs. "I haven't really given it much thought. Maybe in the spring?"

"Really?" I take my phone into the bathroom, put the plug in the bathtub, and turn on both faucets. "Spring is a bit far in the future, don't you think?" The gushing water is loud, so I walk to the kitchen where a bottle of Pinot Gris is chilling in the fridge.

"Well, Lydia. Thanksgiving is coming up and I have to organize my new kitchen. Gary's coming over soon to measure up my units."

"But life's short, Sheena. Carpe Diem." I seize a wine glass from the shelf.

"Excuse me?"

"Seize the day." I set the glass down on the worktop, open the fridge, and locate the chilled wine bottle.

"Yes. Of course."

"So, why not book your ride for tomorrow or the next day?" I open the top drawer and find the corkscrew. "You could perhaps use it as a visitor experience day and get paid while you're on the trek. It's only going to be a couple of hours, and then you can report back and share, firsthand, to the hotel guests." I peel off the foil top and poke the pointy end of the corkscrew into the exposed cork.

Sheena is quiet on the line. "I suppose I could ask."

"Didn't you tell me, one time, that staff get a bonus for being proactive, or some such?" I push then twist the corkscrew into the cork until it's all the way down.

"Ah yes. I'd forgotten about that. I could make this activity fit, and be up for the Outstanding Customer Liaison Officer Award at the end of the year. Ummm. That's something to think about." The line is quiet as Sheena processes the information. I pull out the wine cork which releases with a wonderful pop. Then she says, "Lydia. Will you come with me? The voucher is for two people, and it'd be fun, right?"

"Ah, Sheena." I pour out a glass of beautifully clear, light-colored fruity wine. "I'm a bit tied up. Sorry." I sip, savoring the fresh, tart flavor.

"Oh. Okay. I'll just leave it until you're free." Wine almost explodes from my nostrils. I cough and reach for a paper towel.

"You don't need me tagging along, do you?" I'm still choking, a little bit, but I manage to get my words out.

"You won't be tagging along. We'll be horseback riding, Lydia."

"Yes. Sheena, you are absolutely right." I regain composure and swig a generous mouthful of cool crisp refreshment. "I'm going to arrange my week around our horse trek. Yes. It's important. Good. So, whatever day you decide, is fine with me." The wine has taken effect. I'm suddenly very relaxed. "We're goin' ridin' on ponies. Woohoo! I'm so excited."

"I hope my pony isn't frisky like the one we saw at the demo."

"I don't think they would put an inexperienced rider on an inexperienced horse." I remember my bath water is running, and quickly rush to the bathroom, phone in one hand, wine glass in the other.

"Alright, Lydia. Let's do this thing."

"Yeehaw, pardner!"

elle

"I hope I'm wearing the right clothes," Sheena says as I climb into the passenger beside her.

"Sure, you look great." I yank my seatbelt and click it into place.

"It's just these jeans are a bit tight. It's been a while since I wore them."

"Oh, well, you know denim. It'll loosen up with wear," I say with an encouraging smile.

"Yes. You're right," Sheena says driving on up the street. "And I don't really have any other pants that would be suitable. I only have suit pants that I wear for work. Not really horse-riding attire."

"I think if you're warm and comfortable, that's all that matters today."

"Yes. Rain's not scheduled." Sheena turns to me and grins. "It's going to be an adventure. We're going to have a nice day riding the range."

"It's a couple of hours on a farm track." I laugh.

"I'm just getting into the mood. You know. The Wild West. Wyatt Earp. Kevin Costner. Butch Cassidy and The Sundance Kid. Clint Eastwood. Proper cowboys."

"That's Hollywood Wild West. Reality was very different, I think. Ooh, but I like a cowboy," I say absentmindedly. Sheena makes a turn onto the road, heading out of town.

"You do?"

"Yes. Don't you, Sheena? The hat. The boots. The slow easy walk."

"Yes. I suppose so. There's a certain pleasing aesthetic to a cowboy demeanor."

"And what about Luke?" I ask gently probing for an affirmative. "Do you think he has a pleasing demeanor?"

"He is a very handsome man," says Sheena with a coy smile. "No doubt about that."

I sit smugly in the passenger seat, confident that my work is almost complete in the Sheena/Luke matchmaking department. A few hours saddled up together should seal the deal nicely. It's what they both want. Isn't it? And I've made it my mission to see these people together. And happy.

On reflection, my matchmaking plans haven't gone so well, so far. But I'm positive about the outcome today. I look out of the window at the passing fences and trees, smiling with self-congratulation.

Chapter 16

Luke

Sheena booked the trek for herself, plus one. It's the day before I fly out to visit a possible breeding partner but that's fine. I'm happy to lead the trek. It'll be good to show Sheena what we have to offer the hotel guests and tourists in the area. I'm sure that's her main reason for wanting to win the prize. She is obviously super keen; otherwise, why would she have put her name into the draw so many times?

Ray helps me saddle the ponies, Mabel and Olive. They are quiet and steady, temperaments perfect for first-timers and children. Our pedigree Quarter Horses are separate. For breeding purposes only and for sale.

Ray fits Mabel's bridle, then leads her out of the loose box and into the stableyard to wait for Sheena and her plus one.

She could be bringing a colleague from the hotel. Or she could be bringing a friend. Perhaps a husband or boyfriend. Maybe Molly from the library or Kate from the café. Or, I secretly wish, Lydia from the floristry shop.

I finish fitting Olive's bridle and lead her out to join Mabel who stands patiently with her head lowered and her eyes half-closed. One of her rear hooves is tipped up on end. She looks like she's snoozing.

Soon a car pulls up and parks near the house. I hear the doors open and close and the sound of female voices. I leave the ponies tethered to the post and walk over to greet my guests.

"Howdy, ladies," I say as my heart leaps because Sheena's plus one is Lydia. I instantly relax and feel a rush of excitement at the same time. I take a minute to shake it off, then say, "Welcome back. Are you ready for a ride?"

"Hello, yes," says Sheena brightly. Lydia is more reserved. She raises a hand and says a quiet hello.

"Alright. Let's get you on a horse, then." We walk together to the stableyard where Olive and Mabel stand quietly with Ray who is holding their reins. He tips his hat and nods politely in greeting.

"So, hands up if you've never been on a horse before," I say by way of introduction.

"I have, but it was a long time ago," says Sheena.

"Same," says Lydia.

"There's really nothing to it. The ponies know their job. All you need to do is stay on." I walk toward Olive and Mabel. "But first, before you get onto your pony, you have to say hello. This is Olive. Lydia, she's your pony today. And Sheena, the grey one here is Mabel. She's yours. Go ahead, say hello. They understand." I allow a minute for the ladies to pat the ponies and get acquainted, then I continue. "The next step is getting on, which can be a bit tricky if you haven't been on a horse for a while. Go ahead, if you want. Otherwise, I'll talk you through it."

Ray helps Sheena onto Mabel, and I stand close to Lydia in case she needs assistance. I breathe in her fragrance, a mix of honeysuckle and fresh-mown grass. I have to stop myself from burying my nose in her hair, the smell is so intoxicating.

"I think I need some clues," says Lydia looking at the saddle which is chest-level. "The pony is a little tall, don't you think?"

"No. Olive is the perfect size for you. Don't worry. I'm here to help. First, stand facing the back of the horse. Then bend your left leg and lift your foot into the stirrup."

"Oh goodness," exclaims Sheena from somewhere behind me. "I can't quite bend my knees so much in these jeans. I'm sure they've shrunk."

"No problem, ma'am," says Ray gently. "Perhaps it'll be more comfortable for you to use the steps to get on Mabel." He leads the patient pony to the mounting block by the barn. "Come over here with me."

"Yes. Thank you." Sheena follows Ray and Mabel across the stableyard. "That looks so much easier."

"So, Lydia. Would you like to use the steps, or are you fine getting on here?"

"No. I think I can get on right here, thanks. My pants are stretchy. I can easily get my foot up into the stirrup." Lydia smiles bravely then says, "But I don't know if I can get my other leg up there and over."

"Alright. Let's see if we can do it together," I say gently. Lydia nods. I try to read her expression, but she turns away and looks serious. I get it. Back to professional distant mode. I clear my throat. "Reach up and hold the saddle front and back. Put your left foot in the stirrup. Then, you're going to hop around on your right foot, spring up, and swing your leg over in one easy movement. You can try it by yourself first, if you want. It might take a couple of attempts."

"Okay." Lydia gets her foot in the stirrup, but Olive shifts her weight slightly, which knocks Lydia off balance. She laughs but quickly regains her composure.

"Have another go," I say stroking Olive reassuringly. "Stand still, girl."

"This time," says Lydia with determination. She gets her foot in the stirrup, reaches up, and takes hold of the saddle, then hops around on her right foot but doesn't get the momentum she needs to hoist herself upward. "Phew! It's harder than it looks. I thought I could do this."

"It's rare that a rider gets up there on their first go. It takes practice. Have one more try."

Lydia breathes for a minute and rolls her shoulders back. Then she repeats the steps. She almost gets there, but not quite.

"You want some help?"

"Yes please, otherwise we could be still here when the sun goes down and miss out on the day's ride."

Across the yard, Sheena is on Mabel. "Woohoo! Look at me. I'm riding, Lydia. What are you doing? Use the step. It's super easy."

Lydia looks from Sheena to me.

"You can use the step. No shame in it."

"No," says Lydia. "I want to do it properly."

"Great. So, you do what you've been doing, and I'll put my hands here on your waist, if that's alright, and I'll help you up." My hands fit smoothly around the beltline of Lydia's jeans as if they were always meant to be there. "Teamwork." This time, with a little help from me, Lydia hops and swings her leg over the pony's back. "Awesome. You did it."

"Well not really, Luke. I couldn't have got here on my own," Lydia says with a huge satisfied smile that radiates sunshine, filling me with warmth. I feel bashful and look away.

"I'll go get Deedee, then we're all set."

"You're coming too?" Lydia says with a hint of surprise in her voice.

"Why yes. I'll be your guide today, ma'am." I touch the rim of my hat before walking to Deedee's stable. My horse is ready to go. He kicks his door when he sees me coming. "Okay, calm down, buddy. We're going now."

I ride Deedee out into the yard where Ray is waiting with Mabel, Olive, and our guests. Before we head out, I go through a few safety points and explain and demonstrate the commands for controlling a horse.

"Try and keep your feet in the stirrups. That really helps. Oh, and don't fall off." Sheena and Lydia look at each other, then back to me. I sense some nervousness from Sheena as if she is pre-empting disaster. "Horses are very smart. They pick up on your mood, especially if you're anxious. Whatever you're feeling, they feel it too. So, relax and have fun." Lydia smiles at Sheena who still looks uncomfortable. "We're going up the track behind the paddock to the treeline, and then to the lookout." I point up the hill behind the stable block. "The ride is an hour and a half. Maybe two, depending." I swing Deedee's head around in the direction of the track. "All good to go? Follow me."

Chapter 17

Lydia

Luke places his hands on my waist to help me onto the pony and I lose concentration for a good long minute. His hands are strong and warm and the feel of them makes me quiver. Part of me wants to fall on the ground, giggling, and part of me wants to fling my arms around his neck and cover the man in scorching kisses. But then I remind myself of the point of today. I've set him up with Sheena, so this handsome, capable cowboy remains absolutely out of bounds. Completely. I check my hormones and tell them to get back in their cage. This is not my date with Luke Maddox. This is Sheena's date with Luke Maddox. I am just tagging along. A plus one. If they are going to couple up, they need some time alone together. It's my job to see that that happens.

"This is lovely," says Sheena with a huge smile as her pony follows Luke's horse out of the stableyard.

Our horses' hooves clip-clop along in a relaxed side-to-side amble. I casually look around at the farm buildings and the paddocks where other horses and ponies graze. They lift their heads with twitchy ears, nostrils flaring, and whinny hello as we pass. Then I look back at the stables and the house nestled among trees and gardens. The ranch is deceptively large, extending from the road, behind the house, to a broad green valley that is split into a patchwork of paddocks and trees.

The track broadens out up ahead. I guess it's about wide enough for two horses to walk side by side, which gives me an idea. I reach out and grab a stick that's poking up in the grass beside the track. With a quick tug, it comes away easily in my hand. Then I catch up to Sheena's pony and use the stick, tapping it gently on Mabel's rump. Nothing happens. Annoyingly, the pony doesn't alter its stride at all. So, I go in again, a little heavier this time. Instead of a polite tap, I jab the stick, pointy end, onto a spot near the pony's tail. Instantly, the alarmed little horse neighs, kicks out with its ears back flat on its head, and charges up the track at a brisk trot, almost overtaking Luke.

"Ooh!" Sheena exclaims. "Ow! What just happened?" Her voice is jarred and wobbly with the pony's trotting motion. "Is it meant to be-e-e this bumpy-y-y?"

"Whoa, Sheena. It's not a race," says Luke as she passes him. "Pull on the reins to ask Mabel to slow down."

"Sorry. But I didn't do anything." Mabel slows to a walk again. "She just started running on her own. Maybe she got stung by a bee?" Sheena looks around for a pesky insect. The two horses up ahead fall into rhythm, side by side. I stay behind and allow my pony to chomp leaves and grass that's growing abundantly at the side of the track, quietly congratulating myself on a mission accomplished. I watch the would-be couple interacting. I can't hear their conversation, but it's not hard to fill in the blanks.

Sheena is probably asking about the ranch and the horses Luke's family is breeding. He's probably telling her about his love for animals and how he's been living a bachelor life, but he's come to a decision. He'd like a family of his own. He feels comfortable talking with Sheena about these things because, somehow, she and him are connected. In a moment, he'll stop and reach out for her hand that she will shyly extend his way. Then Sheena will turn to me and say something like, "Lydia. I have a small request. I hope you don't mind if Luke and I go on alone. I know we came out here together for a horseback ride. But..." And Sheena will gaze longingly at Luke then say, "... we're in love now. I'm sure you understand." And I'll say something like, "Of course! I'll see you back at the ranch. Take your time."

"Lydia, are you alright?" Sheena calls back over her shoulder.

"Yep. Couldn't be better."

I'm lost in my own thoughts as trees meet overhead dappling the sunshine in amber, oranges, and golds – glorious autumn colors. The plodding pace of the horses lulls and soothes.

But then, Sheena's pony stops, and Sheena turns to me and says, slightly breathlessly, "Lydia. I'm sorry." She sighs. "Luke. Just a minute."

"Are you okay?" I steer Olive next to Mabel. Luke is up ahead but turns Deedee back toward us.

Sheena blows out her cheeks. Her face is suddenly pale. "I think I've done something to my back." Sheena wiggles in her seat. "When the pony took off, I felt something go ping. And, oooh, I can't get comfortable. And the saddle is rubbing my legs raw."

"Oh, no. That's not good," I say putting my hand around my friend's shoulders. "We'll go back now, huh? We'll come for a ride another time, okay?"

"No. No," Sheena says, lifting her feet out of the stirrups. "I'll get off the horse here and lead it back to the stable. Honestly, walking is preferable to riding."

"Are you sure, Sheena?" I say feeling bad because it was me that made her horse take off. "Hey. We'll all go back. No problem." I'm filled with remorse, and I look to Luke for backup.

"Sure. Let's all go back. It's fine," says Luke calmly. "We can rebook for another day. No problem."

"Luke. Please." Sheena puffs, leans forward, and takes hold of the front of the saddle. She swings one leg over, then slides off Mabel's back. The pony stands still as Sheena slowly eases both feet to the ground with an extended exhaled groan. She steadies herself then says, "Take Lydia up to the lookout. I know she's been dying to see the view." I open my mouth to oppose this idea, but Sheena shuts me down immediately. "Go on, Lydia. I'll be fine. Ouch." She rubs her butt. "By the time you go up and back, I'll be at the car. I'll just walk back slowly in my own time."

"Alright, Sheena. If that's what you want. I'll call Ray to let him know you're on your way back. He'll look after you and, please, make yourself comfortable at the house. There's lemonade in the fridge or tea. Help yourself."

"Thank you. You're so kind," says Sheena trying to smile. "Oh, I feel such a ninny."

"Don't. You're not the first," Luke says reassuringly. "You won't be the last. There's no point in riding if you're experiencing discomfort. It's not possible to enjoy yourself if you're sore somewhere."

Sheena rubs her butt again. She's smiling but knots of pain knit together on her forehead.

"I'm coming with you, Sheena." I kick off a stirrup, but Sheena stops me dismounting.

"Lydia. Stop. I am not a child. Go and have some fun. You deserve it. And don't worry about me. I'm fine."

Luke looks from Sheena to me. "I'd love to show you the view from the lookout. We're more than halfway there now. It would be a shame not to see the ranch in all its fall glory. Why not?"

"Okay. That would be so nice... Sheena," I add anxiously. "Take care. We'll see you very soon."

Luke and I watch Sheena lead Mabel away. She turns and waves then rubs her butt and laughs before walking down the track with a very wide gait.

"Shall we?" says Luke lifting his hat slightly, then repositioning it back on his head. His blue eyes crinkle at the corners in a secret smile that spreads to his lips, and as if he has flicked a switch, I am all lit up on the inside. Luke's smile tells me that everything is going to be alright. I instantly relax and urge Olive to follow Deedee on up the hill.

Chapter 18

Luke

Finally, I'm alone with Lydia. The anticipation of this moment sends me suddenly self-conscious and shy. We allow the horses to take us up the hill in silence. Not that it's an awkward silence because I don't know what to say to her. It's more a peaceful non-speaking silence. We move through the landscape as if we are a part of it. Connected. Tree branches meet above our heads. Leaves, disturbed by the breeze, fall around in yellows, reds, and browns. The wind picks up in gusts. It's chilly. I turn up the collar of my jacket.

"Are you cold?" I ask. The sound of my own voice surprises me. "It can get pretty windy at the top."

"No. I'm fine. Enjoying the fresh air." Lydia smiles and looks up at the sky for a moment, then she says, "Poor Sheena. She was so looking forward to riding today."

"Yeah. It's a shame, but there's always another time."

The horses plod on side by side beneath a tunnel of autumn leaves.

"She's a great person," says Lydia. "So helpful. And thoughtful." Birds chirp unseen in bushes as we pass. "She has a cute house that she's renovating."

"That's nice."

"Yep. She's really good at interiors. You know, putting colors and textures together. She's very creative that way."

I nod, then I say, "You must be creative, though. Working with flowers... and apples."

"Yes. I suppose I am."

"How did the wedding go? Were the crabapples a big hit?"

"Gosh, yes. I have photos. I'll show you." The track narrows into a switchback turn. I push Deedee on ahead. "I had this vision of what I could do with the crabapple branches," Lydia continues. "But you never know exactly how a display is going to turn out until it's done. There's always an element of surprise. That's what makes my job exciting. And a pleasure."

"Cool. So, you have staff to help out?" I ask, turning to face Lydia.

"Oh yes. I have an amazing team. You met Laura the other day when we were pruning your trees. And there's Marty. He's my other flower angel. They are both so talented and trustworthy. And I can call on a couple of friends, if we get snowed under, for odd hours, evenings, and weekends. I couldn't operate my business without help. We have flat-out bookings right through the holidays to next summer." The sun breaks through the scudding clouds, dappling the bare earth of the track. There's a pause before Lydia goes on. "Valentine's Day is probably the maddest day of my year. Although, with summer being wedding season, May to September is pretty busy too. Weddings form my main income stream. People are willing to fork out big bucks for the happiest day of their lives."

"I didn't realize a flower store could be anything more than selling a few bunches of daisies."

"Luke. I might need to educate you, just a little bit." Lydia shoots me her beautiful smile. "Here are some fun facts about the floristry industry." She breathes deeply and clears her throat for theatrical effect. "According to the

National Retail Federation, Americans spend - on Valentine's Day alone - approximately 2.6 billion dollars on flowers. That's just floral arrangements and bouquets, excluding other gifts, such as candy and cute bears."

I whistle my incredulity then repeat, "Two point six billion? That's a lot of cash."

"Yep. One article I read recently, stated that around a quarter of a million roses are cultivated and cut specifically for that one special celebration day of love."

"Maybe I should sell all my horses and plant some rose bushes."

"You could. Or you could plant some roses, but having horses is useful when it comes to fertilizing." There's a beat before Lydia continues. "You have crabapple trees. I'm predicting a trend uptick in decorative crabapple popularity after the wedding I just did."

"Great. Is it too early to plan for early retirement?"

"Not at all." Lydia grins across to me making my heart leap. "Of course, the other crop you may consider supplying is wildflowers."

"Oh yeah?"

"Yeah. If you can, graze your horses leaving a partial strip of the paddock roped off, allowing flower species to flourish. You'll be surprised by what grows without any input from you. I'm always looking out for wildflowers for my store. Not only will you get cash, you'll be helping bees."

"Wow, Lydia. You've given me a lot to think about." We ride on in silence for a few paces more, then something occurs to me. "So, where do all these roses come from? On Valentine's Day? February around these parts is winter, right? And roses? I always thought they bloomed in summer."

"That's right. So, we need to import them from places with a warmer climate. Ecuador and Columbia mainly." The horses have slowed to an easy walk as the gradient evens out. I've let the reins slacken and Deedee takes advantage and nibbles some grass and ferns growing along the side of the track. "And get this," says Lydia. "Rose cultivation is thought to be the unexpected positive spin-off in the war against drugs because farmers are seeing better returns growing roses than coca leaves." Lydia's face is all lit up. "I don't know how much truth is behind that snippet, but wouldn't it be nice if flowers and romance were more powerful than force and weapons? That love really can save the world."

I laugh. "I'd love it if everything was as simple as you make it sound. Almost like a mathematics equation. Love plus roses plus third-world farmers equals no drugs and happily-ever-after."

"Exactly! Isn't it just like that?" Lydia chases a strand of hair away from her face and tucks it behind her ear.

"No. But I wish it was. Life is a lot more complicated, I think. But I'll keep your equation in mind, the next time I buy roses."

"And who do you buy roses for?"

I pause for a second. I'm about to say, "You, Lydia. I'd give you Columbia's entire Valentine's Day export quota, if it made you smile." But instead, I say, "My mom. She loves roses."

We're almost at the lookout. I steer Deedee to a fence-post and jump down. "So, tell me, Lydia. When did people start being crazy in love with roses?" I tie the reins loosely so that my horse can graze. Then I reach for Olive's bridle and lead her to stand beside Deedee. "Why not sunflowers or geraniums?"

"It's interesting. I've done a little research around social traditions and most of the highlights in our year - Christmas, Valentine's Day, Halloween - are inherited from England. And in Victorian times, I'm not sure why, but people became very emotional."

"People weren't emotional before?"

"Well, yes, I'm sure people have always had feelings. But the Victorians really got to work in expressing those feelings. Especially romantic love." Lydia slides off Olive's back and almost into my arms. She takes a step back to steady herself, then she says, "You see it in the artwork. It's very sentimental." Lydia walks a few paces ahead. "Anyway, those Victorians, I'm not sure who, but someone assigned different meanings to flowers. You can Google the Language of Flowers. There's a ton of stuff. So, back to your question, roses mean different emotions according to color. But red roses mean I love you, in the most romantic way. And that idea is accepted everywhere, worldwide." We walk together up a narrow track to the highest point.

"Okay. Here we are," I say as we arrive at a space that I've cleared between the trees with an uninterrupted view down the valley and the surrounding hills.

"Oh my!" Lydia exclaims shielding her eyes with both her hands as she surveys the vast panorama. A gust of wind blows her hair around wildly. Lydia turns to me, her face a picture of sheer joy, and says, "Luke. This is incredible. Thank you so much for bringing me here."

The moment is pure magic. Happiness fills me and I resist an overwhelming urge to take Lydia in my arms and kiss her with every fiber of my being.

Chapter 19

Lydia

The view from the top of the ridge is breathtaking. I say something about love and Valentine's Day roses, then I forget the point of the conversation. The sky stretches out overhead, and I can see for miles in every direction. A wave of happiness washes over me, quickly followed by a slap of guilt that makes me want to climb back on Olive and gallop, full pelt, down the valley, up the other side, and disappear into the trees of the national park.

I regret poking Mabel's rear end. If I hadn't, it would be Sheena up here at the romantic lookout with the handsome cowboy. Today couldn't be more wrong. And worst of all, I'm beginning to believe my own hype about romance and giving into the emotions of a beautiful moment. It would have been easy to make an excuse, to head back to base, giving the would-be love birds a chance to be alone. But selfishly, here I am with Luke, and I am feeling things that I shouldn't.

Luke stands close by, a hand distance away. If I reached out sideways with my pinky finger, it would be so easy to find his, without taking my eyes away from the horizon. My pulse races at the idea of touching Luke's hand. I breathe deeply to calm the emotion threatening to well up and overflow.

What have I become? *Just look at yourself, Lydia.* Am I a Victorian heroine in corset and crinoline? Ridiculous. All that talk about the language of flowers has seeped into my imagination. All that sentimental romantic nonsense is for other people. I remind myself of the reason for coming out here today. And it's not about me. This is not how I thought the day would go. At all. But then, I look out at the fabulous landscape stretched out below and I feel on top of the world.

I sneak a sideways glance at Luke's handsome face, but he catches me, and I blush. I can't help but admire his jawline. His straight nose. The wrinkles at the outer corners of his eyes that make him appear to be smiling all the time. I like the way he sits in the saddle; the way he handles Deedee; the way he moves, as if being on a horse is the most natural thing. I like how he stands; his strong arms loose at his sides; his broad shoulders and deep chest.

I know I've messed up. Today was supposed to have been about Luke and Sheena. Two people destined to be together, with a little help from me. Then maybe, after a romantic ride together to this beautiful lookout, when I ask Luke who he'd give roses to, he'd say Sheena. And not his mom.

However, this could be a good sign. If Luke only thinks about giving roses to his mom, that surely means that he isn't romantically linked at this present time. All is not lost. As long as I don't fall for my friend's intended boyfriend, my plan is still on track.

"We should go," I say with urgency because the distance between us is closing, and I can no longer be trusted to make sensible lucid decisions.

"Sure thing, ma'am," Luke says tipping back his hat on his head, an action so attractive, I turn away and walk back to the horses.

Sheena waves as we clop into the yard.

"That was wonderful, Luke," I say as Olive slows to a stop. "Thank you very much."

"The pleasure was all mine, ladies." Luke dismounts then holds Olive's reins as I swing my leg over the back of the saddle and lower myself to the ground. Luke stands close. I'm aware of his hands outstretched ready to catch me if I fall. I imagine those hands wrapping their warmth around me, making me feel safe. I imagine Luke saying, "Lydia. I got you," which makes me all wobbly. I swat away my foolish imaginings before they cause any more trouble.

"Lydia," says Sheena snapping me out of my dreamy state. "How's your butt? Sore right?" She laughs. "Sorry to have to hurry away, but Gary is due at my place to fit the new dishwasher."

"Sure, no worries."

"Well, I guess I'll see you in the new year, when I get back from Texas," says Luke still holding Olive's reins in his strong warm hands.

"Have a wonderful holiday season, Luke." Being back on firm ground allows me to regain composure. "And thanks for the ride. I loved it."

"Sheena. You need to come back again to see the view," says Luke with his gorgeous smile.

"It's spectacular. It really is," I say with enthusiasm, thinking about how close Luke was standing beside me at the lookout.

"Great. Yes. I'll do that. Perhaps I'll tag along with a group booking from the hotel," Sheena says. "I'm sure that won't be a problem. I'll need to get some better-fitting pants though."

Luke says goodbye then leads Olive and Deedee into the stables. I turn to wave, but I don't think he sees me. It would be nice to stay and take the saddle off Olive and give her a well-earned brush. I'd like to plait her mane and tail, and weave flowers through to make her look pretty.

Sheena and I walk back to the car. "That was fun, Sheena. Thanks for bringing me as your plus one."

"No problem. Glad you enjoyed it. I think horseback riding isn't really my thing."

Sheena and I are almost at the car by the house when I hear Luke call, "Hey, Sheena."

We both stop and whirl around. Could Luke be about to ask Sheena on a date? Has he finally got the courage up to ask to see her again? I watch mesmerized as Luke walks, almost in slo-mo, toward us. My heart beats in anticipation of what is surely to come. Sheena totters back to meet him.

I watch from the car but pretend that I'm checking my phone. Luke is carrying something. He smiles and passes the item into Sheena's waiting hands. I can't hear what they are saying but maybe it's something like, "Would you be free to have dinner with me before I leave for the holidays?" Or, "It was a shame you didn't come to the lookout. I'd like to take you up there sometime soon. Just you and me. What do you say?"

Sheena turns around and walks back, limping slightly. She's smiling and swinging her jacket, which could be a promising sign.

"Silly me," she says getting into the driver's seat.

"What? What did Luke say?"

"I forgot my jacket. Left it there on the fencepost like an idiot." She laughs and starts the engine.

"That's it?"

"Yes. What more is there?"

I can't believe I need to work so hard at this matchmaking business. I'm not getting any help from these two, at all.

Chapter 20

Luke

I lead Olive and Deedee back into the stables thinking about how nice it was to ride with Lydia. She's a natural on a horse. Very relaxed. Not at all anxious. And she's so easy to talk to. I'd like to have more time to get to know her better. She hasn't shared much about herself. Mind you, neither have I. But I love her unstoppable optimism and the way she believes that love can save the world. And that flowers have meaning beyond being pretty. I love the way she gets all caught up when she's talking about things she's passionate about. Her enthusiasm is infectious. I could listen to her all day.

Being with Lydia today has made me reconsider my single status. Am I ready to trust my heart with someone again? I thought I'd be content on my own. But then, since meeting Lydia, all these possibilities occupy my thoughts. I wonder if she's as intrigued about me as I am about her. Probably not.

I spot a jacket draped over the stable door. I'm pretty sure it belongs to Sheena. She was wearing it when she arrived. The ladies are almost at the car, so I call out. They both stop and turn around.

"I think you left this," I say holding up the jacket.

"Oh, silly me," says Sheena almost breaking into a run back to retrieve the item of clothing. "Thank you." She takes the jacket from me. "And I'll be in touch. Enjoy your trip."

"I will. Take care." I wave to Lydia who is waiting by the car. She waves back then gets into the passenger seat.

At the lookout, there was a moment where I thought she was going to reach out for my hand. Then, suddenly, the shutters slammed down again. Why do I feel as if she's holding back? I should just let it go. Try and ignore the attraction that's building between us.

In Deedee's stable, memories of Lydia flood my mind as I unfasten the saddle and slide it off his back. My horse stands perfectly still, patiently waiting to be released from his trappings. I picture Lydia at the hotel when we first met, hiding behind a huge vase of flowers, when I checked in. Then, when she came over to ask for permission to cut branches from my crabapple trees. Then, I remember Lydia at the Old Oak when we danced close to the slow love song. She was sweet and shy, and felt so good in my arms. The connection that night was undeniable. And yet, what happened? It's hard to say.

I brush Deedee with broad, firm strokes until his coat shines like a copper plate. I comb his mane and tell him he's beautiful. He already knows and tosses his head to show me.

It'll be good to get away for a while. I need time to assess the Lydia situation. Perhaps, with time, she'll open up a little more. When I get back from traveling, I'll call her. Ask her out on a date. Go out for coffee. Something like that. Lydia is a puzzling conundrum alright.

———*ele*———

Later, in my room, I'm packing for my trip when my phone rings. It's Dad. He's calling to tell me that he's heard, through the grapevine, that the mare I'm interested in, is hot property.

"You know a quality horse when you see one, Luke," my dad says laughing. "Just trust your gut, okay? Watch her move. She's got to be proud, like a princess. A little attitude is a good thing. But crazy, out-of-control? No. Don't go there. Too much trouble and hard to manage. You'll be making things tough for yourself. But you know all that, Son."

"Yep. Thanks, Dad. I learned everything I know from the best in the business."

"That's right." My dad laughs again. I think that the conversation is over and I'm about to hang up when Dad says, "There's something else I'd like to run past you, if that's okay."

"Sure. Go ahead." I move toward my closet, open the door, and take out a couple of plaid shirts on wire hangers.

"I'd like you to go to Dubai. There's a horse breeder there who has been in touch, but I'd like someone to go and check him out."

"Whoa, Dubai!" I remove the shirts from their hangers and lay them on the bed. The hangers clatter to the floor.

"Yes, Luke. Have a think about it before you make a decision."

"Dad, that's exciting. When?"

"Soon. After Christmas would be ideal, but..."

"Oh, okay. I don't see a problem. I'll just need to organize staffing here at Green Acres."

"Great! So, bring your passport, we'll sort out travel arrangements and you can fly from here."

"Okay, sounds good." I pull open the drawer in the bedside table and rifle around until I put my hand on my passport. I open it up and check the expiry date, then toss it on top of my shirts in the bag.

"We'll talk about it more when you're here."

"Perfect. I'll see you very soon." I'm almost done packing. "Bye Dad and thanks for calling."

"Thanks for picking up." My dad laughs again. "We'll see you real soon. Mom sends her love. She can't wait to see you."

My dad hangs up the call and I gather my toothbrush and shaving stuff from the bathroom. When I return to place them into the travel bag, my phone rings again. I pick up after a couple of rings believing it's Dad again, and he's forgotten to tell me something. But it's not my dad.

"Hey Luke," says a familiar female voice. "I hope this isn't a bad time to call." I freeze, holding the phone at arm's length, deciding whether to hang up or not. I haven't heard this voice for months. "Luke, are you there?"

Chapter 21

Lydia

The spirit of Christmas is alive and buzzing at Blossoms in Bloom. Laura's festive window display showcasing our gift ideas against a floral arrangement of poinsettias, holly, rose hips, ivy, and pinecones, has been a huge hit attracting Christmas customers to our store.

It's Christmas Eve, traditionally, always a busy day with last-minute purchases and general panic buying. I'm digging deep into my reserves of patience as one final customer dithers by the woven reindeer. She picks up one, turns it over in her hands, puts it down again, then picks up another which is almost identical. The clock ticks past closing, and I wonder how long she is going to think about which reindeer to buy.

Marty and Laura peep out from the workroom to check on what is holding me up. I shrug and smile as best I can while willing the woman in front of me to make a decision and a purchase.

"This one is pretty," she says holding up the first reindeer. "But I like the colors of this one." She puts the two reindeer, side by side on the shelf, as if they are pulling an imaginary sleigh.

"Here's an idea," I say brightly, hoping desperation isn't showing through my clenched teeth. "How about you get both? They're so obviously a pair. It would be a shame to split them up. Wouldn't it? How sad would that be?" I pick up one of the reindeer and pretend to gallop it away from its friend.

"Oh, goodness. You're so right." The customer looks sincerely troubled by the idea of splitting up a pair of best-friend reindeer. "Maybe they're in love and will both die of a broken heart if I take one and not the other." Tears well in her eyes. A reaction I had not considered.

"Here's what we can do. Because it's Christmas and you are my last customer for the year. I'm going to give you a special discounted price if you buy both."

"Really? You are so kind, my dear. Well, in that case. Let's take all six. They are so adorable I'm going to have such fun watching my grandchildren unwrap them tomorrow."

"Done." I breathe a sigh of relief. "Let me put them in a pretty bag for you. If you'd like to follow me to the counter."

I swipe the reindeer lady's card and hand over the bag containing her gifts, then I usher her to the door before she sees anything else she may want to buy.

"Happy holidays," I sing as I shut the door, lock it, and turn the sign over to read, 'Closed'. Then I lean my back against the door and send up a prayer of thanks to the gods of retail. Marty is already at the till ringing up and printing the day's takings. Laura helps by counting the cash.

"Nicely done there, boss," says Marty. "Rather you than me."

"I wasn't even sure she was going to buy anything." I tidy the shelves on my way back to the counter. "So many people come in, pick things up, put them down again, and move on their merry way without spending a dime."

"So true," says Laura laughing.

"Alright team, let's do what we need to do, as quickly as possible, then we can tuck into our sweet treats that I've been looking forward to all day."

Marty, Laura, and I agreed not to exchange gifts at Christmas. But we've made a tradition of sharing some Christmas goodies when we close up on Christmas Eve. We each have our specialty and try to outdo each other each year with elaborate and inventive decoration.

Marty is a master of the traditional rich fruit Christmas cake that he steeps in sherry for about a month before shrouding the moist cake in marzipan and decorating it beautifully in snow-white frosting and fun Christmas characters.

"You could go into business," says Laura beaming at Marty's fabulous Christmas cake creation. "Each year they get more bonkers and beautiful!"

"Why thank you, I think," says Marty. "Yeah, but your gingerbread? Yum yum." He takes one of the snowman-shaped cookies from the plate and nibbles off the head.

Our seasonal indulgence is interrupted by a knock on the door. My heart sinks as I immediately assume it's Reindeer Lady back for a refund. But it's Molly.

"Hey, girlfriend," I say opening the door for her. "You're just in time to join our festive feast."

"Only if I'm not intruding," says Molly with a shy smile.

"Not at all. Come on in." I step aside to let Molly in, along with a chilly gust of wind, before forcing the door shut, locking it again, and checking that no more customers are about to barge their way in for that last-minute gift. Molly waves hello to the team.

I haven't seen my friend for a few weeks. She has been away at Cam's family reunion, somewhere in California.

"It was so great to meet everyone," Molly says when I ask about her trip. "But it's nice to be back home." We retreat, out of sight, into the workroom. "I love the festive window display. Whose handiwork is that?"

Marty points at Laura, who smiles at Molly, then arranges our Christmas treats on a length of gift wrap that she has unrolled on the worktable. I present my Yule log, which is average at best this year. But everyone is too polite to say anything about it. I cut the chocolatey sponge roll into slices. But it is buttercream-heavy and falls into sticky blobs. We sit around the worktable on my collection of mismatched stools. We eat and get messy.

"Are you going to the Christmas carols service tonight?" asks Molly partway through a blob of Yule log. "Rev Manvers stopped by the library today with more flyers for the noticeboard. But I think he wanted to make sure that I hadn't forgotten."

"Of course, we'll be there," I say only just managing to articulate because frosting is sticking to my teeth. "And we'll take what's left from here for the after-party in the hall."

Laura offers Molly a gingerbread snowman. "Thanks," she says before biting off a leg. "It's going to be so nice having a few days off."

"Sure is," says Marty. "I'm planning to do nothing. Although, my mom always has a list of things that need fixing when I go over to visit. It'll be nice, though."

"Yeah," says Laura. "Here's to time off..." She raises a piece of Christmas log in salute. "... because when we come back, it's only a few short weeks before we're in hyperdrive, as we get ready for Valentine's Day."

"Hah! Why did you have to say that now?" I moan like a petulant child. "I don't even want to think about it. Let's enjoy the holidays."

There's a break in conversation as we nibble some more, then Molly asks, "How did the horseback ride go? Was it fun?" Molly bites the head off her snowman. "I can't believe I haven't seen you since. What happened with Sheena? I saw her a couple of weeks ago. She was walking very strangely, as if she was in pain."

"Ah yes. I don't think she had a good time," I say sheepishly. "Her pony bolted, and she put her back out."

"Oh, no. Poor Sheena," says Molly concerned. "And how are things going with Luke? Did they hit it off? Swap numbers? What's happening there?"

"Oh, I don't know." I put down the gingerbread snowman that I thought I wanted. Guilt from my part in the pony stampede has changed my mind. I've lost my appetite. "Perhaps they're both too shy, face-to-face, in person?"

"Fair point," says Laura. "I like to chat online before I meet up with potential boyfriends." She takes out her phone and turns it on. "You learn a lot from what a person says in a chat. And what they don't say. It allows you to weed out what you don't want before the awkwardness of going on a date."

"Gosh. Interesting." I prick up my ears. "Are you on... What's that dating app? Timber? FindMe?"

"No. I use this one." Laura holds up her phone to show us an icon on the screen. "TheOne4U. It's good. Easy to use. You just make a profile. You can upload a photo, if you want. Or create an avatar. Then you just type in what you're looking for regarding a date mate." Laura scrolls through some pictures of smiling young men.

"Could you type in something like, cowboy, horse guy, tall, aged 25 to 35ish? Lives around here?"

"Sure." Laura types in some search terms and waits for a selection of possible matches to load.

"Wait a minute," says Molly who is peering over Laura's shoulder. "Isn't that Luke? It looks like him, doesn't it?"

Laura holds up her phone and enlarges the photo so that I can see. "It certainly is a striking resemblance," I say. "What's his name?"

"Well, we don't know what his actual name is, but here on the app, it's Lonesome Cowboy."

"Is he looking for love or just a good time?" asks Marty with a cheeky grin.

"Says here that he'd like to meet a like-minded woman who enjoys the outdoors," says Laura reading from the screen. "Someone who is happy and loves animals."

"Ooh. Come on. We should go," says Molly noticing the time. "The carols will be all sung and finished by the time we get there."

"You're right. Let's wrap the cakes for later. Tis the season to be sharing," I say as I usher everyone out of the store. But then, I hang back, turn on my phone, and download The One4U dating app. I quickly create a profile, but without uploading a photo, and name it, Hotel Babe. Then I message Lonesome Cowboy and wish him happy holidays.

"Lydia. Are you coming?" Molly yells through the open door.

"Yup. Just grabbing my purse," I yell as I switch off the lights, shut the door, lock it, and scurry after my friends who are already halfway up the street.

Chapter 22

Luke

At my parents' house on Christmas Eve, everything is all go. The atmosphere bristles with festive energy driven, of course, by Mom. Typically, she has made more food than a small country eats in an entire year. I asked if she needed some help, but she shooed me away with a tea towel and said that I'd only get in her way. So, I leave her to it. Christmas songs are playing at full volume in the kitchen and Mom sings along to all her favorites. I retreat to the living room where comforting smells of home baking follow me down the hall. I relax into an easy chair and call Ray at the ranch to check in and wish him a merry Christmas.

"I took a group of four up the lookout and they loved it," Ray says with a smile in his voice. "They've posted their review on Tripadvisor. Have a look. It's very positive and they've given us five stars."

"That's great, Ray. The more five-star reviews we get the better."

I'm soon joined in the living room by Maisy who flops down on the couch then kicks her feet up on the backrest. Her phone shines a dim bluish light on her face as she starts scrolling.

Ray fills me in with other Green Acres news. Treasure is doing well, he says. The vet came for a routine check. Everything is normal. Nothing to report. Ray says that things are pretty quiet over Christmas and New Year, and nothing needs my attention before I get back from Dubai.

"Alright, I'll best get going, Luke. There's a Christmas carol service at the church. It's not so much about singing carols, but the shared refreshments afterward. Some people get just a teensy bit competitive with their Christmas cookie decorations. There'll be drama, no doubt. It's always fun."

"Merry Christmas, Ray. Thanks for holding the proverbial reins till I get back."

"No worries. And happy holidays, boss, to you and your family."

Maisy yells from across the room, "Merry Christmas, Ray."

Ray laughs, "Merry Christmas Maisy. I hope you've been good, so Santa brings you something nice." I hang up the call and listen to Mom, down the hall, singing 'Santa Baby'.

I turn my attention to Maisy who is still on her phone, scrolling. "Tell me about your presentation. How did it go? Did you smash it?"

"Oh, yes, I did. Everything went super well. I rehearsed a lot and didn't forget anything. And my course leaders on the panel said they were impressed with my creativity and solutions to real-life problems. The only downside was that I didn't do the swot analysis that well."

"Swat analysis? What is that?"

"Strengths. Weaknesses. Opportunities. Threats. It's a way to assess what needs doing in an organization." Maisy lifts her eyes from the phone screen, briefly. "It was supposed to be more detailed than I made it. But I wasn't marked down that much. I was still placed in the top five percent of my year, so..."

"That's fantastic! Well done, you."

"Thanks." Maisy glances down at her phone again.

"So, what now? What are your plans for next year?"

"Wow." She leans her head back against the cushion. "You know what? I'm going to take things easy, then see what kind of jobs I can get. I may do an internship in digital marketing. That will fast-track me to better pay and more interesting work. In film or music. I don't know. Something fun and creative."

"I'd say from what I've seen, you choose what you want, and you'll pretty much make it happen, Maisy. You're that sort of person."

Maisy smiles at me. "Thanks, Uncle Luke. That means a lot."

"If you want, you could help out at Green Acres while I'm away in Dubai."

"Paid?"

"Yes, paid." I laugh. "Have a think about it. The horses still need exercising, and you could run the online stuff. That would be a huge help."

"Gosh, Luke." Maisy sits up straight and looks directly at me. "You really trust me?"

"Yes. Why are you so surprised. You did an amazing job with Green Acres's online presence. You know the business side of things, and you know horses. But most of all, you're family. So yes, I trust you. Do you think I'm wrong?"

Maisy collapses sideways with laughter. "No. You're not wrong. And I will take you up on your offer, if the terms and conditions are beneficial."

"Terms and conditions?"

"Well, yes. We're family but we also need to be business-like. If I'm working for you, then I'll need a job description."

"Are you messing with me?"

"Yes. Haha." Maisy swings her legs back up onto the couch and giggles. "I love it at Green Acres. I'm happy doing whatever. Just leave me a list." We're quiet for a moment then she says, "So how are things going with the pretty lady from the hotel?"

I think carefully about what Maisy is asking. I'm not about to give away any secrets. "What pretty lady from the hotel?"

"The one who came to the ranch when I was there." Maisy looks at her phone again. "She was asking about apples or something."

"Oh, yes. Actually, she came along to the Open Day with some friends." I try and steer the conversation back to safe ground. "It was a good day."

"Did you get her number?"

"No. Why?" My niece is relentless.

"Luke. You are so annoying." Maisy stares at me then dramatically rolls her eyes to the ceiling.

"Sorry, Maisy. You've lost me."

"Alright. Let's put it another way. Are you dating anyone at the moment?"

"No. I'm here having Christmas with my loving family," I say through gritted teeth. "Don't you ever quit?"

"Can I ask you a question?"

"Sure. But you may not get an answer."

"Alright. Here goes. Are you still hung up on Courtney?"

"Maisy. We broke up ages ago. She's history."

"Ah, yeah. That's what I thought. But..." Maisy is distracted by her screen again. "Oh, never mind."

"Never mind what?" I concentrate on not reacting to Maisy's 'fishing' game: hook 'em and reel 'em in. I refuse to be hooked.

She takes a deep breath then says, "Okay. This may not be news, but I saw Courtney at the mall, and she says that she's looking forward to seeing you and..." Maisy pauses for a second. "Luke."

"Yes, Maisy."

"You're not thinking about getting back together with Courtney, are you?"

"It baffles me, Maisy, that you think I want to share my relationship details with you. Or anyone for that matter."

"It might help to talk, you know. Clarify what's going on."

"Don't worry. I'm clear. But thanks for wanting to be my therapist. I don't need one. Just yet."

As I say this, Maisy's phone beeps. Her eyes widen and dart to the screen. Then she turns back to me. Her nose twists to one side in thought. "Excuse me, one moment," she says swinging her legs down to the floor. She stands up and leaves the room.

_ _ _ _ _

"It's so nice to see you, Luke," Courtney says close to my shoulder as we stand at the bar we used to come to when we were together. It hasn't changed much, if at all. But it feels strangely unfamiliar. I look around at the pretend rodeo-style interior and wonder why we ever came here. Visiting now after months away, I see how fake and shoddy it all is. The walls look like they're made of solid timber, but the beams are just tacked on and the antique-looking light fittings are missing some bulbs. Loops of sad dusty tinsel are the only giveaway that it's holiday season. I'm almost one hundred percent sure that they never come down in between Christmases. Apart from Courtney and me, there are only three other people in the place.

The barman nods to me in recognition. He's wearing a Santa hat. "What'll it be folks?"

"You know what I like, Luke." Courtney tilts her head and bats her eyelashes at me. "Don't tell me you've forgotten."

I turn to the barman and place my order. "One Paloma and a Modelo, thanks."

"I'll bring them over, if you want to find a table, sir, ma'am."

Courtney leads me to the corner table. "This used to be our table. Do you remember, Luke?"

I nod and sit down, but not too close to Courtney. We wait for our drinks which the barman brings on a tray with a plate of dry roasted peanuts, a stack of red serviettes with cartoon snowmen dancing around the edges in cowboy boots, and a mobile card payment terminal. I tap my bank card on the machine which spits out a receipt. The barman rips it off and hands it to me with my card. Then he takes the tray back to the bar.

Courtney raises her cocktail glass and waits for me to raise my beer bottle to clink a toast. We each take a sip, then Courtney says, "So, how have you been?"

I lean back in my chair. "I've been fine. In fact, I've been more than fine, Courtney. Moving to Oak River was the best decision of my life."

"Oh?"

"Yes. I love the ranch. The horses. And the people are pretty cool too." I drink some beer. "And what about you? How's L.A. working out for you? Do you love it?"

Courtney sighs and shakes her head slowly from side to side. "No. Not really." She looks down at the table where a ring of condensation is forming at the base of her glass.

"Oh dear. I'm sad to hear that."

"Are you?" She shoots a narrow-eyed glare at me. "I thought you would be happy to know that I'm miserable."

"Why? Why on earth would I be happy to know that you are miserable, Courtney? What kind of person do you think I am?"

"Look, Luke. I'm sorry for running out on you. You didn't deserve that. You are so much more than I gave you credit for." Courtney gulps her drink halfway down the glass. "I. Am. Sor-ry."

"Gosh, Courtney. I don't know what to say."

"Say that you want me back, Luke." Courtney gabbles at full speed. "Say that you still love me. Say that we are worth another chance because I believe that we're perfect together."

"Whoa. Stop right there." Courtney is breathing heavily. I can see that she is close to tears. I hand her one of the dancing snowman serviettes. "It's like this, Courtney." I choose my words carefully. "I was hurt when you left. No doubt about that. It was a lesson in heartbreak alright." I pause to sip some beer. "And I appreciate our time together. But I have moved on. In so many ways. And if you're honest with yourself, you'll see that you have too." I smile kindly at my ex-girlfriend.

I don't wish any bad feelings between us. When she called me to say she wanted to see me, I didn't know how I was going to react when we met up. But now we're sitting here together, in the place that we used to love, I feel absolutely nothing for the woman sitting beside me. It's as if we are strangers in an airport departure lounge.

Courtney dabs her eyes with a corner of the snowman serviette, careful not to smudge her heavy eye makeup. "Well, that's not what I expected at all," she snaps. Then she coughs to clear her throat and knocks back the remains of her cocktail. "Wow. Oh, boy." She blows out hard.

"You'll be okay, Courtney." I stand up to leave.

"Wait, Luke." Courtney looks up at me. "I need to borrow some money. And I was wondering if you could help me out." She presses her lips together and waits for my response. I sit down again.

"Are you in trouble?"

"No. Nothing that bad. I just need a couple of hundred to get by until my check clears."

I open my wallet and pull out the notes tucked inside. "Here you are, Courtney. Merry Christmas. Give my regards to your folks. I hope you get what you want."

"I'll pay you back, Luke. This is just a loan, right?"

"It's a gift. No need for payback." I stand to leave for a second time, and I make it to the door without turning around to see if Courtney is watching. The bartender nods as I exit.

Chapter 23

Lydia

After setting up the profile on The One4U on Christmas Eve, I sent a Happy Christmas message to Luke, aka Lonesome Cowboy. I didn't use Sheena's real name, of course, but chose Hotel Babe as the handle that would most certainly leave no doubt in his mind as to who was reaching out to him.

A surge of exhilaration rushes to my fingertip as I press the green OK button. And, yet a niggle in the back of my mind whispers something about the dishonesty of my actions. However, I ignore the irritating niggle because I know that my motivation is noble, and the outcome will be so unbelievably romantic.

I picture the wedding. At the church, probably. In hues of delicate pinks, purples, and blues. With an abundance of lilac for fragrance and texture. And for the hero arrangement? Something very pretty. Not roses. Peonies. Yes. Peonies of the palest pink nestled in lush trailing variegated ivy. I sigh contentedly at my beautiful inner wedding ceremony as a reply pings back almost immediately.

I'm excited to think that these two gorgeous people, who have been too shy to connect in the real world, have now met and can chat online. And then, when they are ready, they can meet up; go on a date; kiss; get married; move in together; have ten or eleven babies; and live happily ever after.

I giggle inwardly when I read the next message from Lonesome Cowboy. 'I've been thinking about you... a lot.'

Alright. I can play this game. 'And I've been thinking about you.' Send.

<hr>

Christmas Day comes and goes. Then it's New Year's Eve. It's a quiet one this year. I'm over at Molly and Cam's place with Dex and Meryl and their kids. After several exhausting rounds of Twister, the kids have gone to bed leaving the adults all rung out and flopped on the furniture. I'm not sure if any of us are going to be awake at midnight to welcome the New Year.

So far, I haven't told anyone about my dating app setup. But when Molly and I are in the kitchen, tidying up after dinner, I accidentally let it slip into the conversation.

"Are you kidding?" says my friend, eyes wide. She leans against the countertop for a minute, her eyes on the ceiling. Then she faces me square on, hands on hips, staring at me as if I had stabbed someone she loves.

"Nope." I keep drying the plate that I'm holding with a tea towel, even though the plate is already dry. "But it's working," I say deflecting Molly's negativity.

"What do you mean, 'It's working'? How can it be working if you're pretending to be someone else?"

"Ah, yes." I'm ready for this argument. "But it's only temporary. I'm only pretending to be someone else until Sheena and Luke go on a date, and then I can delete the profile because it won't be necessary anymore." I add my dry plate to the stack on the counter.

"Do you know how mad that is?" Molly puts a stack of plates away in a cupboard. "And probably illegal... immoral at best."

"How? I'm just giving love a helping hand, that's all."

"Lydia. I know you are doing this for the best reasons but seriously, think about it. You are stealing someone's identity," Molly hisses. "It's just not right."

"Fair point, Mol. But I feel I owe it to Sheena because of what happened on the horseback ride."

"What happened on the horseback ride?"

"Okay. So, this is going to sound mean, and I really didn't want her to hurt her back, but when I poked Sheena's pony's butt, I didn't expect it to take off like it did."

"You poked Sheena's pony?"

"Not hard, Molly. All I wanted to do was to get her pony to catch up with Luke so they could have a nice romantic horseback chat."

"No!" Molly looks incredulous. Her hands cup her face. She looks like a Halloween mask.

"Yes," I assure her. "So, in recompense for my accidental sabotage on that occasion, I have the perfect no-fail romance plan that is going to seal the love-match deal. For real. And whatever little subterfuge I may have used on this gorgeous couple, they'll forgive me in an instant, when they fall in love." I hold the tea towel to my heart.

"What plan?" We have both stopped tidying up. Molly appears to be in shock.

I lay my tea towel on the table, turn to my friend with an award-winner's smile, and announce, "A Valentine's Day date."

"Lydia. Are you absolutely sure you are going about this in the right way?"

"Yes. Molly. Trust me. It's going to be perfect. Just you wait."

As I say this, my phone beeps in my back pocket. Molly raises her eyebrows and waits for me to check the message.

"Ah, it's from Luke," I say reading his words from a faraway land. "He's wishing me a happy New Year and is looking forward to seeing me when he gets back. How nice."

"Wait a minute. Was that to you, or to Sheena? Was it sent to your phone, or through the dating app?"

"Oh, yes. It was to me on my phone."

"Well, Lydia, don't you think that's a bit odd? I mean, it looks like he's a player, doesn't it? Messaging you on your phone and Sheena on the dating app?"

"No. Not really. Luke and I are most definitely in the friend zone. That message was a friend's message. He's probably zipped out a whole bunch all at the same time to everyone on his contacts list." I nod sagely. "You should see what he writes to Sheena on TheOne4U. Phew! Sometimes they're so spicy I blush when I read them."

Valentine's Day

Surreptitiously, I watch Sheena enter The Half Moon Café from the doorway down the block. I feel like a spy. I suppose I am. But in a good way. I have devised a little rendezvous for two people deserving of love. What is wrong with that? Still, the fact that I pretended to be someone else on social media is fraudulent, borderline illegal. Probably. There's a name for that, isn't there? Catfish? Something like that. Sounds negative and underhand. Something I choose to sweep under the carpet as I bury my head in the sand. My motivation is from a good place. But whichever way I frame it, I can't help feeling like a criminal awaiting trial.

Ignoring my pesky inner thoughts, I casually walk around the corner, out of sight, pulling up my coat collar around my ears and my woolly hat down so it almost covers my eyes. Once I've turned the corner, I stop and peer back around so I can keep an eye on the café entrance.

I don't wait long before Luke appears. He must have parked his truck on a different street because he walks in from the opposite direction. I didn't think of that. He could have parked right here on this street, where I'm hiding. My heart beats fast, and I'm short of breath at the thought of Luke surprising me and having to explain why I'm peering around a street corner. Luke stops outside the café and looks up and down the street. So, tortoise-like, I pull my head further into my jacket collar.

I fully appreciate that Luke is out of bounds, but I can't help but admire the aesthetics of the man. He truly is a wonderfully put-together human being. His broad manly shoulders carry his heavy winter coat like a Milan catwalk model. He moves with ease and grace. I like his hair; the way he sweeps his fingers back through his forelock. I should like to sweep my fingers through his hair. The idea causes a warm glow, and I feel my cheeks redden. Still, he's not for me.

I can imagine Sheena at the specially prepared table in the corner. Kate and I arranged everything this morning and she was so helpful and excited by my cunning plan. I decorated the walls with decals of pretty hearts and cupids and made a beautiful table arrangement of perfect red roses with a delicate scent. I even iced two cupcakes for Kate to bring to the table with their coffee order. I get tingles just thinking about the romance I've created.

My phone rings. It's Sheena. I pick up. "Hey, Sheena," I say brightly, expecting a gush of breathy enthusiasm about her surprise date. "How's it going?"

"Hi, Lydia. I'm just checking in. Did we arrange to meet at eleven? Or have I got things wrong? Only it's a quarter after and a..."

"Oh. Yes. Um." I need to think quickly. "Sorry. I've been held up. I'll be there soon. Five more minutes? Sorry."

"Ah. Yes. Look, Lydia. I've got to get going. So sorry that we didn't get to have a catch-up this time."

"Really? Sheena." Why was she talking to me? Why wasn't she in deep and meaningful conversation with the gorgeous cowboy? I almost voice this thought but think better of it. Instead, I say, "I'm sure you've found someone who you'd rather have coffee with than little old me."

Sheena laughs. "I'm not sure what you mean."

The sledgehammer of reality finally hits me. I cough and change my tone. "No. No, I'm sorry, I should have called."

"It's fine, Lydia. Honestly. Another time. I needed a coffee anyway and, Kate's made some special Valentine's cupcakes. So cute!"

I want to ask about Luke, but what's the point. I'm not even sure they said hi. Cupid's job is so hard. I feel defeated. Deflated. Foolish. Foolish and dishonest to the point where I need to come clean. Fess up.

I hang up the phone, leaning my back against the cold, hard wall. My plan did not go to plan, and I'm annoyed. I'm almost annoyed enough to march around to The Half

Moon and grab Sheena with one hand, drag Luke to her with the other, and yell, "Don't you know how lucky you are to have found each other?"

A hot angry tear leaks out from my eye. I wipe it away with the back of my hand. When I look up Sheena is standing right in front of me.

"Lydia?" She looks concerned. "Are you alright? Are you crying? What happened?" She looks around wildly. "Have you been mugged? Assaulted?"

"Sheena! No. I'm fine. I'm okay."

"You don't look okay."

I take a deep breath. "This is going to sound a bit weird."

"I'm listening."

Slowly, instinctively, I begin to retrace my steps back to Blossoms in Bloom. Sheena walks beside me matching my funerary pace.

"Today is Valentine's Day," I say, although it sounds like a sigh.

"Yes, it is," Sheena says brightly. "You're right."

"The most romantic date on the calendar." Sheena nods and squeezes my arm. I glance at her sideways and see that she's grinning from ear to ear. Maybe her date with Luke wasn't a complete disaster after all? "Sheena!"

"Yes."

197

"Are you in love with Luke? Did you have a romantic date just now in The Half Moon?"

"No. What?" Sheena stops dead in her tracks, and I swing around to face her quizzical expression. "Luke was there, but he said he was waiting for his niece."

"Really?" I exclaim, perplexed. "That's not what was supposed to happen."

"Lydia. Is there something you need to tell me?" Sheena links an arm through mine. "But before you do, I've got to let you in on a little secret." We begin to walk again. "I have a date."

I gasp. "Sheena! Who with?"

"Gary from Gary's Kitchens and Bathrooms."

"Really? Gary? But he's..." I picture Gary from Gary's Kitchens and Bathrooms, a short stocky man with piggy eyes and a belly that hangs over his belt.

"Perfect. I know. I'm so excited."

"Gosh. When did...? What?" I realize that I'm too confused to say anything, and it doesn't matter because Sheena is going on and on about her date with Gary, from Gary's Kitchens and Bathrooms, that I can't fit one word in.

"I've wanted to tell you for the longest time, but I needed to be sure. While Gary has been fitting my kitchen, we became quite close. I held back because I didn't want to chase him away. So, I've been waiting for him to make the first move; for him to wake up and see that we are meant to be together." Sheena stops walking to hug me. I'm stunned into silence. "Lydia. I am so happy." Sheena releases me and we continue down the street. Sheena links her arm through mine again. "So, what was it that you were upset about?"

"Nothing. Absolutely nothing. Just a speck of dust in my eye." I pull myself together enough to say, "I am so happy for you. Really."

Sheena hugs me again and says she's got to run. And I'm left standing on the sidewalk feeling as if I don't know anything anymore.

Chapter 24

Luke

The Half Moon Café is quite busy but Kate waves to me as I come in and seems intent on showing me to a corner table where Sheena, from the Oak River Hotel, is sitting which strikes me as a bit odd as there are other tables that are free.

"Howdy, Sheena. I hope I'm not intruding." I loosen the scarf from around my neck. It's invitingly warm inside compared to the chilly street.

"Hello, Luke," Sheena says looking surprised. "How nice to see you. I'm waiting for Lydia. She's late, unfortunately." Sheena looks around the walls. "Isn't this lovely? Someone's gone to a lot of effort. Kate's very creative. Look at those beautiful roses. Did you ever see anything more romantic?"

We admire the flowers and the wall décor of hearts, ribbons, and little pink angels shooting arrows.

"It's very pretty, but I won't disturb you more, Sheena."

"No. Please. Sit down. I'll call Lydia to find out where she is." I stay standing.

Kate brings two cupcakes decorated with pink frosting and red hearts. "For you sweet people." She beams as she places the plate between us with two forks on folded heart-covered serviettes.

"Oh, how lovely," says Sheena. "Is this a Valentine's Day special?"

Kate doesn't answer but winks and smiles warmly before hurrying back behind the counter where a family is waiting to be served.

I look around at the other tables in the café and notice their lack of themed decoration. Maybe this is the only Valentine's Day table? I'm feeling awkwardly uncomfortable as if I'm the center of attention.

Sheena hunts around in her purse and locates her phone. "I hope nothing serious has happened. Lydia made a point of telling me not to be late." She shakes her head and dials a number.

While Sheena talks on her phone, I call Maisy, but the call clicks straight to voicemail, so I hang up. I message her instead. "Hey, Maisy. Where are you? Should I order coffee or are you going to be some time?"

Sheena is still talking with Lydia, but she waves a hand indicating that I should sit down. Maisy has been held up somewhere, no doubt. So, I take off my jacket, drape it over the back of the chair that's entwined with loops of pink glittery hearts, and relax into the vacant seat opposite Sheena as she hangs up the call.

"It's been so nice running into you, Luke. But I've got to go now. I have a date. With a special someone. A Valentine's Day date." Sheena puts her phone into her purse and prepares to leave. "If you see Lydia, tell her I'm sorry I missed her." She stands up. "Next time."

Sheena grabs her coat and purse, then wraps one of the cupcakes in a serviette. "They just look too good, don't they?" Then she briskly makes her way to the exit.

I'd love it if Lydia walked through the door right now. I could share the solitary cupcake with her. Maybe she would have time for a coffee. But Valentine's Day is a florist's busiest day. She would be rushed off her feet, I imagine. I could stop by her store with a takeout coffee and the cupcake. Would that be weird? Would she think I was trying to...

My phone beeps. It's Maisy. She seems surprised to hear from me.

"Luke! Are you having a lovely time?" she asks. Her voice is strange and pitched higher than normal.

"Yes."

"That's so great! Did you get the special Valentine cupcakes?"

"Um, yes."

"Is she still there? Are you going on another date?"

"Is who still here?" I lower my voice and shift my phone to my other ear. My elbows are on the table. "I was meeting you, right? Or don't you remember?" There's quiet on the line. "Maisy. Are you still there?"

"Yes."

"Do you want to explain what's going on?"

"No."

"I think you should."

"Alright. But I'm at Green Acres. I'll see you back here?"

"Aren't you supposed to be having coffee with me here at The Half Moon Café?"

"That was what I told you, wasn't it? But I said that just to get you there so you could meet up with the woman you like from the hotel."

"Sheena?"

"Is that her name?"

"Maisy. I'm very confused." I sigh heavily. "I'm hanging up now. But I'll see you later."

Something tells me that I've been manipulated in some way, but I can't quite join all the dots yet to get the big picture. Maisy has been reckless and clueless in the past, but after working with her on the Open Day event, and while she's been helping out the past few weeks, I believe she has a good heart, and she only means well. We've mended our bridges, and I don't think she would betray my trust. However, ...

To take my mind off trying to unpick a conundrum which is, quite frankly, giving me a headache, I wrap the remaining cupcake in a serviette and take it to the counter where Kate looks concerned but doesn't say anything. I order two cappuccinos to go. I pay for the coffees and cupcakes.

"Just the coffees, thanks," Kate says as I tap my bank card on the machine. "The cupcakes were a gift."

"Ah, how nice. Thanks."

"Don't thank me. Thank Lydia." My face must have shown exactly what I was thinking because Kate adds, "Lydia Lane, from Blossoms in Bloom, the florist?"

"Yes. Thanks, Kate. I'm going there now. One of those coffees is for Lydia. Do you know how she likes it?"

Kate smiles and nods. She makes the coffee, froths the milk, and spoons the foam on top. She adds chocolate and cinnamon, then fixes lids onto the take-out cups, and gives me a brown paper bag for the cupcake. I leave the cozy warmth of the café and stride with purpose a few blocks to Blossoms in Bloom.

I'm excited to see Lydia. And, secretly, I'm pleased that Maisy let me down, although there are definitely questions that need to be answered. But later.

At the florist's door, I stand aside to allow a middle-aged couple to exit before I go in. Stepping inside Blossom in Bloom is like entering a fragrant botanical paradise, a world away from the winter street outside. Laura is at the counter. She smiles and welcomes me to the store.

"How may I help today?" she says.

"I was hoping to see Lydia. Is she in today? I bought her a coffee." I hold up one of the take-out cups. "Or I could just leave it for her, if she's too busy."

Laura asks me to wait one minute and disappears through a doorway to the office, I presume. Still holding the coffee cups, I gaze around at the various colors and shapes of the petals and leaves in buckets and baskets. A huge wicker heart, threaded with red roses and feathery ferns dominates the window, blocking out most of the weak winter daylight. Happy Valentine's Day banners adorn the wall behind the counter. Gift cards, ribbons, and wrapping paper add to the Valentine wishes.

"Luke!" Lydia sounds surprised. "How lovely to see you." She walks over toward me as I hold out one of the coffee cups.

"It's a cappuccino. Chocolate and cinnamon, but no sugar. That's right, isn't it?"

"Ah, coffee! Thank you. Yes. Perfect." Lydia tears off the lid and lifts the cardboard cup to her pink lips. "How did you know?"

"Kate knows. She made it. I told her it was for you. And this..." I pull out the brown paper bag from my pocket containing the cupcake. "... this is for you."

Lydia blushes and takes the brown paper bag from me. Then she calls for Laura.

"Can you please mind the store for a few minutes, while I have my coffee?"

"Sure thing. Marty's delivering the final orders and should be back soon, so take your time."

I follow Lydia through the doorway to a workspace where, I guess, most of the arrangements and displays are created.

"Ah, the nerve center of Blossoms in Bloom," I say with a smile. Lydia offers me a stool beside a tall wooden table. She perches on another near the corner. Our knees almost touch. "I hope I haven't caught you at a busy time."

"No. Not at all. Your timing is perfect, actually." Lydia sips her coffee. "Thanks for bringing coffee and whatever's in here." She nods at the brown paper bag.

"That's my pleasure," I say as Lydia tears open the paper package. She hops down to retrieve a knife from the bench by the sink where a clear, plastic dome covers more pink frosted cupcakes. Lydia returns and, with one swift movement, slices the cupcake in two, right down the middle of the red fondant heart. The two vanilla sponge halves fall apart and deep raspberry jam oozes from the central wound.

"Happy Valentine's Day, Lydia. Although, I'll bet you've been flat out creating romance for other people." I drink more of my coffee. "Kate, at the café, said that it's you who I should thank for the cupcake." As I reach out to take one of the delicious-looking sweet pink halves, my gaze drifts to the plastic dome again. "Do you bake for The Half Moon, as well as run a floristry store?"

Lydia sips her coffee and appears to be deep in thought. Her eyes are agitated. They dart from me to the cupcakes under the dome. Then Lydia utters something like, "Shoot," under her breath. Her pretty mouth twists to one side. She takes a breath and sighs it out before speaking.

"Luke. I have a confession to make. And I hope you won't think the worst of me."

"How could I?" I laugh. "What could possibly be that bad?"

"Well, I'll explain, and then we'll see."

Lydia's seriousness puts an instant stop to my jovial mood. "Alright. What's on your mind. Tell me?"

"I'm Hotel Babe."

"Excuse me? Who?"

"Hotel Babe is the name I used on TheOne4U dating app." Lydia looks at the floor and kicks a stray leaf that has yet to be swept up.

"Nope. Nothing yet. You're going to have to explain some more." She lifts her gaze and looks confused.

"We've been chatting."

"We have?"

"Online. On TheOne4U." Lydia puts down her coffee cup, hops off the stool, and locates her purse on the bench. She shuffles items around before she finds her phone and turns it on. "Here," she says. "You're Lonesome Cowboy."

"Nah. That's not me. I think you have me confused with someone else."

"But you came to the café to meet me. I mean, Sheena."

"Lydia. What's going on? Sheena was there, but I didn't arrange to meet her."

"No. You arranged to meet Hotel Babe."

"Sorry. I didn't arrange to meet Hotel Babe either. I was at The Half Moon Café because I was..." My sentence trails off as the penny drops. "... meeting Maisy." I put my coffee cup down on the tabletop and stand to leave. "Lydia. I suspect that someone has been playing a prank on both of us. And I'm pretty sure I know who. I'm truly sorry, but I'm going to deal with it right now." I can't believe that Maisy would do such a thing. It's unforgivable to pretend to be someone else. To manipulate. To lead someone on. Then it occurs to me. "What do you mean, I arranged to meet Hotel Babe? I thought you said that Hotel Babe was you. Why did you say that I arranged to meet Sheena? Is she also Hotel Babe? How many are there?"

"Alright. I can see how this looks and, believe me, I had the best intentions. I really did." Lydia stands up and takes a deep breath. "I pretended to be Sheena because I thought you liked her, and she liked you. She's been unlucky in love, so when you walked in at The Oak River Hotel, it was like, Pow! You are so handsome and charming. I thought I could, you know, aid the path of romance for you guys."

"Aid the path of romance? But why?" I start pacing. "Don't you think that people can find love on their own?"

"Well, sure. But sometimes they need a helping hand."

"What? Manipulation? Ambush? Stealing someone's identity? That's illegal by the way."

"It's not like that. I only had your best interests at heart."

"Did you? Did you really? Because a cynical person might look around and wonder, mmm, 'Why is a florist matching couples up?' Because it's good for business? Possibly?"

"No. I mean, yes. If everything goes to plan. The couple might fall in love and want to get married..."

"Goes to plan! Just listen to yourself for a minute. That's the most conniving, manipulative thing I've ever heard. Are you a puppeteer pulling strings all over town? Is that what you do for entertainment?" I shake my head and stride to the exit.

"Luke. I can see how the situation looks but..."

"I'm disappointed. Lydia. I really like... liked you."

"You liked me?" Lydia rushes over and bars my way. "You never said anything about that or gave me any indication that it was me you liked. Why didn't you ask me on a date or something?"

"What?"

"If you'd shown me any kind of attention or given me any kind of a clue about your feelings for me, none of this would have happened."

"Unbelievable," I say, hitting the middle of my chest with my fist. "You're blaming me for your botched match-making setup?" Exasperated, I step past Lydia to the door. But then, I stop and turn around to face her. "And you have been so hard to read. It's like, one day, I think you like me, and the next, you're pushing me away." Lydia's jaw drops open. "And that message I sent from Dubai, about wanting to see you, and spending more time together. Did you not think that maybe, that was me telling you I think you are wonderful?"

"But..."

"I'm sorry. This conversation is over. I'm going now."

Chapter 25

Lydia

When Luke leaves, I stand where I am for the longest time, unable to move. The full force of what I've done hits like a ton of bricks. I've been so obsessed with plans for matching Sheena, I've been blind to what is right there in front of me: the possibility of more slow dancing with the gorgeous Texan cowboy. I slump down onto one of the stools at the table, fold my arms, bury my head in them, and weep.

Laura knocks on the door. "Everything alright in there, Lydia?" she asks tentatively from the other side.

"Yes." I lie. My voice is muffled in the shirtsleeves of my folded arms.

"Okay," says Laura. "Just checking." There's a brief pause. Then she says, "Marty's here. And I'm going out for lunch now. Can I get you something?"

"No. I'm fine. Thank you, Laura." I wipe tears from my eyes with the back of my hands. "I'm just tidying up in here. I'll be out in a minute, okay?"

I sit up and blink away the remaining tears. Then I hunt for a Kleenex in my purse. I can't face anyone just now. The thought of being in the store, wishing happy Valentine's Day to loved-up customers, twists a knot of pain in my stomach. I'm nauseous. I'm miserable. I want to die. I find my phone and dial Molly's number.

"Molly," I sniff.

"Yes."

"I messed up. Big time." I sigh heavily and slump forward onto the workroom table again.

"Hello, Lydia." Molly's voice is even and sensible. Just what I need. "Wait one sec. I'm just walking to my office." I hear her saying something, then a door closing and noises of furniture being moved. "Tell me. What happened?"

I take a deep breath and launch into my sad tale of woe. My friend doesn't interrupt me as I retell the day's disaster, and what should have been the most romantic coffee date imaginable at The Half Moon Café.

"The more I tried to explain things to him, the more I sounded completely mad. Everything that came out of my mouth just dug a deeper hole for me to jump into. And the worst thing of all is…" I choke on a sob. "I really like Luke." I whimper. "I've blown any chance for me and him now." I start crying again. "I hate myself. I'm so stupid."

"You're not," says Molly in her soft, kind way. "You're a wonderfully romantic idealist who wants everyone to be happy and in love."

"That's not how Luke sees me. He thinks I'm a crazed manipulative witch, whose only motivation in getting couples together is, that it's good for business and hope-fully, according to him, they'll get married, and I'll get rich doing the flowers at their wedding. Wah!" Tears pour down my face.

"Gosh, Lydia." Molly's tone changes to high-pitched harsh. "Is that what you've really been up to this whole time?"

"Molly!" I cough and choke and sniff shocked at my friend's question. "How could you think that of me?"

"Relax, friend," Molly says. "I'm just teasing."

"Well don't. I'm not up to it." I slump. "My heart is broken. I'm a big hot mess. And I'm so embarrassed."

"Ah, Lydia. I did try to warn you." There's a pause in conversation then Molly asks, "Does Sheena know?"

"No. No, I don't think so. When I saw her after she left the café, she wasn't interested in listening to what I had to say because she was too excited about her romantic Valentine's date with Gary, from Gary's Kitchens and Bathrooms."

"Oh my!" Molly exclaims. "Gary?"

"I know. He's about the most unattractive man I can think of..."

"No, wait. There are more unattractive men than Gary from Gary's Kitchen and Bathrooms. I can think of a whole bunch."

"True. Yes. You're right. But Molly, we're off topic here." I slide off the stool and walk to where the cupcakes nestle beautifully under the plastic dome. At any other time, I might be tempted by the delicious, pink-frosted sweet treat. "Molly. I think I've learned a vital and important lesson." I reassess my decision to resist a cupcake, lift the lid, and pull one from the stack.

"What's that?"

"There's no accounting for taste." I bite into the soft, vanilla sponge and lick the raspberry jam that oozes out and threatens to plop onto the floor. "We think Gary is maybe a four or five."

"He's no looker, that's for sure. I'd go with three," says Molly. "But alright, a four on a good day when he has just had a haircut and trimmed his mustache."

"Well, Sheena thinks he's a ten. Possibly higher if you heard the way she was talking about him earlier."

"What he lacks in physical attributes he makes up for in personality, maybe?" says Molly.

"Yes, you're right. Gary probably has some excellent qualities, but my point is..."

"Beauty is in the eye of the beholder?"

"Exactly. One size does not fit all and... I thought I was good at matching people." I take another bite into the squishy butter frosting which tastes like romance is supposed to feel. "I'm never going to do that again." The words are stifled in a mouthful of sticky sweet cupcake.

"Sorry, Lydia. I missed that last bit."

I swallow my mouthful and shout into my phone, "I AM NEVER MATCHMAKING EVER AGAIN."

"That's what I thought you said." Molly laughs down the line.

"Hey, do you want to come over to Blossoms? I have cupcakes to trade for a hug."

"Of course. And you don't need to bribe me with cup-cakes. I give free hugs, whenever I can, to miserable friends who have messed up, big time. I'll see you soon."

Chapter 26

Luke

By the time I arrive home, I'm not angry anymore. However, I need to let Maisy know that I am not at all amused by her interfering skullduggery and underhand manipulation. No real harm was caused, but what she did and how she did it, can't just be brushed aside as if it doesn't matter. It does matter. Oh, yes. Maisy pretended to be me. She stole my identity. Online. And that is not cool. At all. I park the truck and stomp up the steps and into the house, jaw set, brow knitted with displeasure. Maisy greets me in the hallway.

"Kitchen. Now." I bark without slowing my stride. I march through the doorway and down the corridor. I pull out a chair at the kitchen table and stand behind it. "Sit," I say looking directly at Maisy.

My niece shuffles over and sits meekly, head bowed. I briskly pull out another chair, beside hers, and sit down. Maisy braces herself, waiting for the storm to hit.

"So, Maisy." I keep my voice steady and even. "You've been pretty busy lately, haven't you?"

Maisy visibly relaxes and says, "Yes, sir. I've updated the website with new photos of the horses and facilities here at Green Acres and set up a brand-new Welcome page, a Contact Us page, and made navigation easier." Her words gabble, double speed. "My next project is to sell branded merch online. You know, caps, t-shirts, hoodies, mugs." She checks off items on her fingers. "It's amazing what you can print on these days. There's so much stuff."

"And..." I fix my niece with a long hard stare. "... you set me up on a date with..." My fingers tap my chin for dramatic effect. "... let me try and remember... Hotel Babe?"

Maisy presses her lips together forming a hard horizontal line. "Luke. Let me explain about that."

"Oh. I am all ears." I lean back on the kitchen chair spreading my hands wide on the table in front of me. "Please, Maisy, take your time."

"I did it for you, darn it," my niece says with unexpected ferocity.

Maisy's harsh loud retort catches me off guard. "For me?"

"Yes, for you." Maisy blows out audibly and slaps both hands on her knees. "Luke. You're one of the saddest people I know."

"I'm not sad."

"Don't interrupt me. I'm not done." Maisy stands and begins pacing. "When Courtney left for L.A., she broke your heart." She stops pacing close to my shoulder. "I understand that."

"She didn't." I lie. A defensive reaction. "I was upset, yes..."

"Please. Don't interrupt me. You'll have your chance in a moment," Maisy says with surprising authority. "Courtney isn't good enough for you, Uncle Luke. She never appreciated who you are. Courtney never saw you. The real you. It's like you were filling in until she left town, or something better came along. I don't know. It's like you were keeping her from being alone." Maisy sits down again, her elbows on the table. "But you gave her your heart. That was plain to see," she says in softer tones. "And then, she trashed it. That was plain to see too." Maisy leans back and takes a breath. "But it's time you got over her."

"I am over her."

Maisy sighs. "No, you're not." She slides forward onto one elbow and looks up at me her head supported on an upturned hand. "Luke. What did you tell me when Spider threw me that day? You said, 'Get back on that pony, or you'll lose all confidence and the next time it'll be harder to get in the saddle.'"

"That's right. I remember. And, Maisy, I was so proud of you when you dusted yourself off, grabbed those reins, and hauled your ass back onto Spider." I smile at the memory. "You showed that grumpy old pony who was boss."

"Yeah. My butt was so sore. I was bruised black and blue for weeks." Maisy laughs, then she coughs and returns to serious mode. "My point is this, Luke. It's your turn to dust yourself off and get back in the metaphorical saddle, buddy."

"You sound like an old person."

"Sometimes it feels that way." Maisy shakes her head and laughs again. "I lived fast and loose for a while and I guess I owe you, and about a million other people, an apology for being less than considerate."

"Less than considerate? Is that what we're calling theft, deception, betrayal, and fraud these days?"

"Alright. You have a point." Maisy stands up and paces up and down. "Luke. I was an out-of-control felon teenager. I wronged you. I stole, lied, and wrecked your car. And I am truly sorry." She sits on the chair beside me and takes my hand. "Please. Forgive me."

"Shucks Maisy. You are the hardest person to stay mad at."

"Is that you forgiving me?" She looks at me quizzically.

"Yes, you idiot. I forgave you long ago. You were just a messed-up kid. And apart from this recent misdemeanor of stealing my identity and setting me up on a bogus date, I'd say that you're alright."

"Wow. I'm 'alright'. Luke, sometimes your emotional outbursts overwhelm me." Maisy gazes at the ceiling. There's a beat, then she follows in a cheery tone. "So, what are we going to do next?"

"What do you mean, 'next'?"

"Your sad empty love life, Luke!" Maisy stands and begins pacing again. "You're an above-average-looking guy. Some might even call you handsome."

"Thanks. I think."

"And the woman who I saw, the one with the apples; the one who has been messaging you on TheOne4U as Hotel Babe..."

"Wait a minute? Hotel Babe, the Crabapple Lady?"

"Yes." Maisy sits down again. "Honestly. I thought she was perfect for you." Maisy sighs out hard, then she says, "And what did you do?"

"What do you mean?"

"See. You are so incredibly annoying. You don't see what is right in front of you. I'm telling you, Luke. A woman like that is not going to wait around for you forever."

"Maisy. I have just been talking with her and..." I pause as I'm aware that I'm about to share something deeply personal with someone I've always thought of as my enemy. "You might think that she's perfect for me, but her motivation for matchmaking me on the dating app is purely for financial gain. She gets couples together because she wants them to get married, so she gets the lucrative wedding design contract."

"Really? I didn't get that impression."

"Maisy. Think about what it is you are saying. You were pretending to be me, and she was pretending to be another woman. So, how could you possibly draw any conclusions regarding character or personality based on communication that is utterly fraudulent?"

"Just a feeling."

"A feeling?"

"Yes."

"Do you know how nuts that sounds?"

"I can see your point, but I think she's nice. And I think she's really into you."

I realize that this conversation is going nowhere. We sit in silence for a good long while until Maisy says, "How did you feel about Hotel Babe before today? Before you found out that she has been pretending to be someone else?"

"Alright, Maisy. For the sake of clarity, Hotel Babe, the one you saw with the crabapples that day, her name is Lydia, and she owns the florist shop in town."

"Right." Maisy nods and smiles dreamily. "So, back to my question."

"How did I feel about Lydia before today?"

"Uh-huh."

"I liked her."

Maisy jumps up as if she has been electrocuted. "I knew it!" She dances around the kitchen then places both hands on the table, as if she's a defense lawyer in a courtroom, and says, "There now, Luke. So, what are you going to do about it?"

"Nothing! I'm going to do nothing because she's a crazy person who I don't want to be within a mile of. She is obviously in need of some medical help." I walk to the kitchen door and an exit from the discussion. "She'll probably be arrested very soon, and I don't want any part in her ridiculous charade." Maisy opens her mouth to say something, but I cut her off before she can articulate her thought. "Enough, Maisy. I mean it."

I walk out of the kitchen and down the hall. I'm going out to ride Deedee to try and make sense of everything. The walls are closing in and I feel as if I'm suffocating. But Maisy follows and catches up with me.

"Okay. Just one more thing then, and I'll zip it up for good." She mimes sealing her lips together with a zipper then crosses her heart.

I look at the floor, then back to Maisy. "What? What do you have to say, Maisy?"

"Just this. You like her and she likes you." I'm about to walk out, but I stay and listen. "Crabapple Lady may have created a hoax that went horribly wrong..."

"Yes. But..."

"Just listen."

"Okay."

"If that is the worst, most terrible thing about her; if trying to set up a date is the worst thing that she has done, then, it's not so bad, is it? It's misguided, for sure. But personally, I don't think her motivation was financial. I think she did it for love." I don't answer. I study the corner of the door where the paint is flaking off. "Luke. I stole your car. I went on a hedonistic rampage without a thought for anyone else." I flick a glance at Maisy. "And you found a way to forgive me."

"That's different."

"Is it? Different circumstances. Yes. And different relationship dynamic. Okay. But the sense of betrayal is the same."

"Man, you are so annoying."

"But I'm right, aren't I?" Maisy grins at me, her hands on her hips, as if she has scored a point. "She's perfect, Luke. Call her. Give Crabapple Lady a chance."

I don't say anything. I take my hat off the peg in the hall and walk out of the door.

Chapter 27

Lydia

I t's been a few weeks since the Valentine's Day debacle. My head is still reeling from the scene in the Blossom in Bloom workroom. The murdered cupcake lying split open on its side, oozing raspberry jam; Luke's handsome face and the look of disappointed disbelief as he turns around and leaves; me, trying to say things to make him understand, but each word digging a deeper hole for me to fall into. Although the scene replays randomly throughout my day, the sense of shame diminishes, slightly, each time. But I'm still left feeling full of remorse, empty, and stupid.

Keeping busy helps to take my mind off the painful memory and refocus my mental energy. I've thrown myself into work and reorganized my workroom, clearing out any unused props, vases, and other bits and pieces that I once thought would be useful, but are just sitting around collecting dust. And, with the Oak River Annual Spring Fair only a couple of weeks away, I put my hand up for extra duties. Mrs Radley, the fair's coordinator, was effusive with gratitude and even hugged me after the committee meeting.

"You are an absolute gem, Lydia," she gushes as other committee members pass us and noisily make their way to the exit at the community hall.

"It's a team effort, Mrs Radley." I force a smile as I know I'm making myself do extra as penance for my huge mistake in meddling with other people's hearts. "I'm happy to help, where I can."

"This year is going to be the best yet," says Mrs Radley with a smile usually reserved for celebrities or the mayor. "We have great people in our little town. Really great people."

"Yes, Mrs Radley," Molly says as she grabs my elbow and steers me toward the door, rescuing me before Mrs Radley launches into her Small Town: Big Heart speech. "I think you're right. It is going to be the best fair yet."

"Thank you," I whisper as we leave the community hall. We wave goodbye to the remaining committee members and continue on our way.

Molly laughs. "What for, this time?"

"For rescuing me and for being my friend."

Molly links her arm through mine. "You would do the same for me."

"You wouldn't be such an idiot." We walk across the town square. "You're far too smart."

"To be honest, Lydia. I'm a bit concerned that you're not looking after yourself." Molly stops walking and faces me. "Your sparkle has gone. You look terrible."

"I feel terrible."

"Hey. It's still early. Let's go to The Half Moon. We haven't seen Kate for ages. Come on. Why not?"

The café is warm and welcoming. Soft soul music plays to customers chatting quietly at a few occupied tables. Kate waves over from the counter where she's making coffees and frothing milk. She calls out to Dylan in the kitchen, to come out and take our orders. Molly and I install ourselves at our favorite spot by the window, so we can look out at passersby, although the lamplit street is deserted.

"This is such a good idea," I say looking at the chalk-board menu. "I forget the healing power of cake and girl-chat."

Dylan comes over with a pencil and order book. He greets us with his easy lopsided smile. "Evenin', ladies. The specials today are the lasagne served with mixed salad, and the Thai-style chicken served with jasmine rice. Sorry, we're out of ribs until tomorrow." Dylan waits, pencil poised. "What can I get you?"

Molly and I consider our options for a moment. "It all sounds amazing, as usual," says Molly perusing the list of food options.

"I'm going for the triple chocolate layer cake with cream and extra chocolate sauce, please," I say without need-ing more time to decide. "And a large mochaccino with marshmallows and sprinkles." Dylan nods and scribbles on the order pad.

"And I'll have the salad of the day, thanks, Dylan. And a spirulina. Yeah. I think that's all." Dylan repeats our order back to us then smiles and returns to the kitchen.

Molly leans across the table and takes both my hands in hers. "You need to stop beating yourself up. Enough is enough."

"I know, Mol." I sigh. "But the memory of Luke's face, when he left my store, hurts me to my soul."

"Well, you are not going to change anything by feeling bad about it. Acknowledge your mistake. You messed up. I told you so. But move on. Lydia. It's time. I want my friend back. Not this sad excuse for a person who's sitting opposite me right now. It's boring."

"Okay. You're right." I smile weakly. "Triple chocolate cake helps."

"Alright, but you do realize that chocolate cake, in this instance, is not food. It's feel-good medication you are using to try and make yourself feel better."

I shrug like I'm a teenager then blow out my cheeks. "You're right, Molly... again. But it works. Chocolate cake does make things better. But only while I'm eating it. Afterward, I'll feel yuck and I'll be in toxic shock for a couple of hours. I'll probably get a headache from the chocolatey sugar-loaded stimulant and I won't be able to sleep."

"How about we balance things out." Molly smiles kindly. "I'll trade some salad."

I laugh. "You always balance things out. You're such a good friend."

"I'm not kidding. This is the last time." Molly's expression switches to something more serious. "Get yourself together, girlfriend. You need to turn things around."

Kate brings our order on a tray. She sets down the mountainous plate of rich, dark layered chocolate cake with everything on it; the beautifully colorful crispy salad; the steaming chocolatey mug, brimming with cream; and the deep green healthy spirulina in a tall glass, wet with condensation. Kate puts two sets of silverware wrapped in serviettes on the table beside the plates of food. The café has emptied out, so she pulls up a chair and joins us.

I launch into the delectable sweet, sticky feelgood chocolate medication. "You want some?" I say with a mouthful.

"No. Thanks. I'm all good." Kate says smiling at me. Conversation is minimal as noises of appreciation replace actual words. After a while Kate says, "Lydia. What I don't understand is, why you didn't think Luke was for you? It was so obvious that you were attracted to each other. Everyone else could see it." Kate looks at Molly to back up her statement. Molly nods and sips her healthy drink.

"Kate's right. The way Luke looked at you. Wow," Molly says with her head on one side. "And it was crystal clear the effect he had on you, girl."

I put down my chocolatey spoon and look from Kate to Molly and back again. Then, I reach for the spoon again but change my mind. "He's just so handsome." The chocolate-induced headache has kicked in early. "And kind. And, gosh, his eyes." The cake effect is making me emotional. "And now, there's no way he is ever going to see me other than a manipulative witch."

"That may be," says Kate. "If he does, or if he doesn't, you can't dwell on it anymore."

"When you finish this plate of cake and mug of mochaccino and walk out of here, you need to be Lydia again, okay?" says Molly.

"Is this a what-do-you-call-it? An intervention?" I ask, wiping tears from my eyes and chocolate sauce from my chin.

"Something like that," says Molly. "It's what friends do."

Chapter 28

Luke

At the Spring Fair, I watch Lydia from a distance. She's laughing with a bunch of people who mill around her in the marquee. She's so pretty. Like a butterfly, so natural in her element. The center of attention. Everyone loves her.

The contestants in the flower arrangement competition all wear expressions of anxious relief – brows knitted; thin smiles; tired eyes. They have each presented a creative display on one of a line of tall round tables, under a sign which reads, Floral Design Competition. It'll soon be time for judging.

Unexpectedly, Lydia raises her gaze, and her eyes meet mine across the sea of heads. She smiles and waves. Her smile lassoes me with its friendly warmth. I'm caught. She pulls me to her through the crowd. The distance between us narrows and suddenly I'm right in front of her.

"Hey, Lydia," I say because any more words elude me.

"Luke. It's so great to see you." Lydia reaches up to kiss my cheek. The feel of her soft lips lingers on my skin radiating a glow that spreads throughout my body, making my fingers and toes tingle. "How do you like the Annual Spring Fair?"

"It's really loads of fun. I had no idea it would be this popular." Lydia's eyes twinkle and make me forget what her question was. "I'm having a great time. Thanks."

"I knew you would," she says as someone close distracts her attention from me. "Excuse me one sec." Lydia holds up an index finger. "Don't go anywhere, okay?"

"Okay."

I stand to the side, where I hope I'm out of the way, and watch the proceedings of the floral arrangement design competition. Lydia speaks into a microphone and addresses the onlookers. She welcomes returning visitors and first-timers to the Annual Spring Fair, then introduces the judges and expresses her admiration for the contestants.

"Once again, I feel relieved that I'm not a judge this year. I couldn't possibly choose a winner. But luckily, we have a panel who are more than capable and have volunteered to take on the challenge of choosing Best in Show."

An avalanche of applause and cheers ring around the marquee followed by a reverential hush as one of the judges accepts the microphone from Lydia.

"Thank you, Oak River Spring Fair committee, and to the brilliant Lydia Lane of Blossoms in Bloom for organizing this wonderful event," says the short, stout woman wearing dungarees and her hair scooped up in a scarf. "It's been a tough decision. But we have an overall winner." She waves a white envelope around her head before opening it and pulling out a folded piece of paper. "The judges were impressed by use of color, texture, and form with this arrangement. The contestant has been brave, imaginative, and extended the collection of stems, blooms, and leaves to a harmonious symphony greater than the sum of its parts. It gives me huge pleasure to award this year's Best in Show prize, of a one-hundred-dollar garden voucher, to..." The judge struggles to open the envelope while holding the microphone. It's clear that she's excited. Someone steps in to assist. She coughs, swallows, and takes a moment before she announces, "John Jacobson for his creation, Dawn of Time!"

A man standing behind a display of long woven leaves and exotic-looking deep red flowers grasps his chest with both hands. John Jacobson, I assume. He is hugged from all sides before making his way to the spokesperson with the microphone. He seems too overcome with emotion to speak. But eventually, he mumbles some words of thanks into the mike, before accepting the envelope and a hug from the short stout woman.

Lydia appears by my side. We join the rest of the crowd in tumultuous applause as John Jacobson waves the envelope and then disappears behind a wall of well-wishers.

"That was intense," I say close to Lydia's ear. I can smell her perfume, a heady mix of floral fragrance and vanilla. Lydia mimes that it's too loud to hear and pulls me toward the exit and fresh air outside. "I've never seen anything quite like that," I say once we're clear of the clamor.

Lydia beams. "It's something else, isn't it?"

We stand face to face in the crowd - a flowing stream of bodies moving past us, up and down.

"So, what's next?" I ask filling the gap in conversation with a question. "Do you want to grab a coffee? Or maybe something stronger?"

"A coffee. Yes." Lydia laughs. "I might get too giddy if I give in to my need for a cocktail right now."

"We can't have that," I say, captivated by Lydia's laugh.

She steers me to the nearest coffee cart which isn't far away, although we need to negotiate the crowd and weave through the oncoming people traffic. Safely at a seating area, we find a vacant picnic table. I go to the coffee cart window and place the order before returning to sit opposite Lydia.

"Lydia." I have rehearsed what I want to say, over and over, in my mind. But now it's time to voice my thoughts they seem scrambled and unclear. "I like Oak River."

"That's good. Oak River likes you, Luke Maddox."

"It's been a positive move for me," I continue without prompting. Lydia holds my gaze and smiles encouragement, so I go on. "Lydia." I repeat her name as if it's an anchor.

"Yes, Luke. Really? No regrets about taking on Green Acres?"

"No. I mean yes. What I'm trying to say is, I'd like to see where things go."

"Oh yeah?" Lydia looks at me with a wide-eyed stare.

"At the farm, you know, with the trekking and breeding program and the horse stock."

"Oh. Right." Lydia lowers her gaze to rest on the table-top. "Horse breeding."

"And, I'd like to see if..."

The barista calls out that our coffee is ready, so I pause my thought and walk over to collect two cardboard cups, serviettes, and a massive chocolate brownie that looked too good to miss. I return to our picnic table.

Lydia takes one of the cups, "Thank you, Luke. And, yay for the brownie. They're really good here."

"Have some. I bought it to share." I break off a corner of the chocolatey treat and offer it to Lydia.

"Thanks, but I'm off chocolate. It reminds me of a bad experience." Lydia winces, then sips a little coffee. She places the takeout cup on the wooden table in front of her and leans forward on her elbows. "You were saying?"

I suddenly feel self-conscious as if the whole direction of my life is about to change according to the reaction I get. I clear my throat and sip my coffee to compose myself. Then my phone rings and my heart sinks.

"Sorry. I need to get this."

Lydia looks toward the marquee, and I'm scared she's going to walk away, so I reach out to touch her hand. She smiles and says, "It's fine. Go ahead."

Ray is on the line. He bypasses pleasantries and jumps straight to the point. "Treasure has gone into labor, boss. I've called the vet. He's on his way."

"Thanks for letting me know. I'm coming right now. Tell her not to have her baby until I get there, okay?" I laugh to keep things light, but my heart is pounding like a freight train. A mare in foal is risky at the best of times. But Treasure is in labor ahead of schedule. She could lose the foal. And, worse still, we could lose Treasure.

"I'm sorry, Lydia. I have to go. My best mare is about to give birth. And it's early."

"Oh, wow! You must," Lydia says concerned. "Yes. Yes, of course."

I stand up abruptly as my brain kicks into work mode. I orientate myself, trying to remember where I parked the truck.

"Listen," I say instinctively patting my pocket to locate my keys. "Do you want to, maybe, come with me?"

"Yes. Yes, I do," Lydia jumps up. "Gosh, if you're sure."

"I'm sure. But come on." I reach for Lydia's hand. "We've got to go right now."

Chapter 29

Lydia

I was so surprised to see Luke in the marquee at the Floral Design Competition. And even more surprised when he asked me to go for coffee. He seemed pleased to see me. It was like a dream. We sat at a picnic table. Things were going well. We chatted about this and that, and then I felt he was going to tell me something important when his phone rang. It was Ray, his stable manager, telling him that his prize mare, Treasure, was going into labor.

I thought that he'd rush off and leave me, but then, more surprise, Luke asked me if I wanted to join him. Of course, I jumped at the chance. I've never been at the birth of anything before. What an honor to be invited. I hope I don't faint or throw up. He holds my hand as we hurry through the crowd to where Luke parked his truck. We jump in and before I can process what's going on, I'm sitting up front in Luke's truck, and we're driving out to Green Acres.

I feel a bit apprehensive. We don't talk much on the drive up to the ranch. I can only imagine how Luke must be feeling. I sneak a sideways peek at Luke. He drives steadily. His face is serious. I text Marty, asking if he and Laura can manage packing up after the Floral Design Comp. He texts me back straight away with a smiley face emoji and a thumbs up. He has a key for the van and says he can drive it back to base for me at the end of the day. I text back a heart and breathe out a relieved sigh.

As if he's concerned with how I might be feeling, Luke says with a smile, "Are you alright? Almost there. I hope Treasure's okay." There's a beat before he says, "Thanks for dropping everything and coming with me."

"Hey. No problem. Thanks for asking me. It's quite humbling to be invited to witness a birth. And I've messaged my team. They are going to pack up after the event.

I'm so lucky. They are very capable. They can probably run the entire business without me."

"Oh, I'm sure that's not possible, Lydia. You're the life and soul of Oak River."

My chest contracts with emotion at Luke's kind words. Even after the Valentine's Day disaster, Luke can still see good in me. No one has ever called me the 'life and soul' before. 'Pain in the butt', yes. 'Life and soul', no. I clench my jaw to squash a sob down where it belongs and blink away tears to stop them leaking out. I'm way too emotional. Maybe it's because of the foal about to be born, or being whisked away by a gorgeous cowboy, who calls me ma'am; who, until a couple of hours ago, I thought hated me. I don't know. All this drama is creating an urge to grab Luke's leg. But I resist for fear of causing an accident.

We drive on without speaking for a few moments more, then Luke says, "I've been wanting to call, Lydia."

"Oh yeah?" Luke flicks a glance at me, but his eyes quickly dart back to the road ahead.

"I'm not a complicated man. I like things to be simple." I nod encouragement but I don't interrupt. "That whole dating thing, when you tried to set me up with your friend. Well, I felt like a wild mustang caught in a pen. I was cornered. And I didn't like it." Luke looks at me briefly again. "Now. Don't get me wrong. I believe you may have had the best intentions."

"I did. That's right. Misguided, I admit. But my motivation came from a good place."

"I see that now. And I've had time to..." Luke's sentence is cut short by his phone ringing. "Sorry. It's Ray calling." He taps the green square on the screen of the dashboard to answer the call. "Ray, talk to me."

"Luke. Just checking where you are," says the voice on the line. "Treasure's waiting for you but the baby wants to make an appearance."

"I'm through the gate. See you in five," says Luke before he hangs up the call.

Luke steers the truck through the ranch gate and up the driveway to the stables. He cuts the engine and jumps out. Then he comes round to my door and offers me his hand, which makes me swoon. But I pull myself together. This is no time to be mushy. A baby horse is being born.

Chapter 30

Luke

Treasure is uncomfortable. She snorts and sweats. I brush her side with handfuls of hay and talk softly to her about how beautiful she is. The mare paws the ground and whinnies plaintively, then snorts some more and walks around her stall. I can't do anything more for my prize mare. It's all up to her now. I leave Treasure and join Lydia and Ray who watch from the other side of the gate.

"The vet should be here soon," Ray says quietly, more to himself than to me.

"Are you worried?" Lydia asks clearly concerned for the distressed animal pacing around the stable.

"Nah. Not yet. She's a good mom," I say calmly, although there's always a chance of mortality even with the best vet on site. "This is not her first foal. But it's good to have medical expertise standing by. Just in case. There's a whole raft of things that could go wrong if she can't manage on her own."

Treasure circles the stall, kicking up hay. Her belly is taut, stretched wide by the leggy offspring due to be born any second. The mare blows and grunts. She circles once again, then lies down, her nostrils flared, her eyes wide, her breathing short and shallow.

Ray's phone rings. "The vet's here. He's in the yard," he says. "I'll bring him in." I nod and Ray hurries away.

I watch Lydia who hasn't taken her eyes off Treasure. She is caught up in the moment, willing the animal to relax and for her pain to cease.

Ray is back soon enough and introduces the vet. Efficient and business-like, formalities are brief. The vet carries his bag into the pen and strokes the mare's neck. He puts on plastic gloves and checks her temperature. Then he examines her rear end.

"She's doing well. Nicely dilated," the vet says. He looks at his watch. "I say we wait. Give it fifteen, twenty tops."

It's midnight when the vet leaves. The foal is suckling, standing next to his mother on wobbly skinny legs. Treasure turns to sniff and groom her new baby. She is as proud as any mom could be with her beautiful boy. Finally, I feel confident I can leave them for the night. Ray says that he'll check in on them every hour, just to be safe.

"Are you sure? We can alternate, Ray. No problem," I say although I'm beat.

"I won't sleep, Luke. So, I may as well be here at the stable keeping an eye on things. You go and get some rest. I'll report anything that happens, but it all looks swell so far. She's a good mom. You can tell. And that little guy. He's a future champion." Ray smiles. He's tired but happy.

I say goodnight to Ray and shake his hand. Then, I put my jacket around Lydia's shoulders and lead her slowly out of the stables, through the yard, and back to the house. She cries the whole way. Silent tears. I guide Lydia up the steps, onto the porch, and sit her down on the swing seat.

"That was the most wonderful thing I've ever seen in my whole life," she says between sobs. "I'm sorry. I'm just a bit overwhelmed. It was just... so real. So beautiful. And the little foal. So... helpless." I hand Lydia a box of Kleenex that I retrieved from the truck. She takes a couple of sheets, blows her nose, and wipes her tears.

"It's alright," I say gently. "I think I was the same when I first saw a foal being born. The miracle of life puts everything into perspective, doesn't it? And you're right, it is the most wonderful thing."

We sit side by side on the swing seat. The night is quiet. A big old full moon hangs fat in the sky, shining down on the valley stretched out beyond the crabapple trees.

Lydia sniffs and I hand her more Kleenex. She takes another and I leave the box on the cushion beside her.

"I'll get some water. Do you want anything? Something to eat, maybe?" Lydia shakes her head. I slowly stand up. "Alright. I'll be right back."

Without turning on any lights, I find a jug on the shelf in the kitchen and fill it at the sink. Then I place it on a tray with two glasses. The moonlight is bright enough for me to see. I walk out to where Lydia still sits, where I left her, on the swing seat. I set the tray down on the side table, pour the water, then hand one of the glasses to Lydia.

"Thanks," she says. Her teary eyes shine. We sip our water and listen to the natural noises which fill the night air.

"Lydia. I'd like to talk about something I was going to share earlier."

"Okay, Luke. I think I know what you're going to say." Lydia moves to the corner of the swing seat. She looks small and timid in my jacket. Holding her glass in both hands in her lap, she bites her lip and gazes at the floor.

"When I last saw you...," I say from the other end of the seat. "... I maybe overreacted."

"No. I don't think you did. Gosh. I can see how everything looked from your side," says Lydia. "What I did was unforgivable. Really. I don't know." She turns to face me. The moon has sculpted her features in silver. "I get an idea in my head and run with it without thinking things through." She laughs. "Luke. I'm sorry." Her eyes search mine in the moonlight, pleading with me. "I am so sorry."

The woman in front of me is so perfect I melt. I let out a long sigh. "Lydia." My shoulders relax. I resist a need to reach out and hold her. "I was angry. No doubt about that." Lydia shrinks visibly into the cushions. "But I believe your intentions were good. Even though you went about things in the most ridiculous messed-up way."

"Yes. I know. Things turned so bad." Lydia takes a moment, wipes her eyes, sniffs, and turns away. "Listen, Luke," she says sliding closer to me, still sniffing. "I know you must think I'm about the worst person alive, but I'm not. I would love it if… " Lydia sighs.

"Firstly, I don't think you're the worst person alive."

"You don't?"

"No. I've had time to process stuff. And here's what I think…"

"Okay, let's hear it."

"I hope you don't think that I'm judging you. I'm not." I stare out into the semi-darkness of shadowy trees and bushes. "I believe you have a good heart. That your motivation is from a place of love. You didn't mean any harm to anyone. And I don't really believe you tried to match me with your friend as a business prospect."

Lydia smiles at me and visibly relaxes. "Luke. You don't know how happy hearing you say that makes me feel. Do you think that maybe we can move along and… be friends?"

"Friends? Yeah, we could start by being friends for sure. But Lydia…" I turn to face her in the moonlight. Her eyes still glisten with tears among the shadows of her face. "… when I came to Oak River, I was here to fulfill a purpose. I had a job to do and that was that. I had no idea that I would get so caught up… emotionally. With you."

"With me?" Lydia says with incredulity.

"Oh, my. It's been so frustrating," I say slowly shaking my head. "All this time, I've wanted to ask you on a date. But then, I'd get all these contradictory messages. I'd feel as if you liked me one minute, and then you'd start talking about Sheena and saying how much she was into me. Look. Sheena's nice and everything, but she doesn't light me up the way you do."

"I light you up?"

"Yup."

"Luke." Lydia says, scooting over a little closer to me. "You light me up too." She sips more water from her glass then sets it down on the table. "So, did you want to slow dance with me at the Star Rangers gig?"

"Oh, yes. I really did."

"And did you want me to win the horse trek voucher at the Open Day, so we could ride to the lookout together?"

"Uh-huh."

"And did you want a romantic date at The Half Moon Café, at the corner table with raspberry heart cupcakes?"

"No. Not really. That's not my thing." I reach for Lydia's hand and hold it in mine.

"What I really like is something more like this." I gaze around at the serenity surrounding us. The trees, the stars, the moonlight. "I've pictured us just like this. On the porch in the moonlight."

"Luke," says Lydia, her head tilted to one side. "I am such a dummy."

"Yes. This is true."

"Would you mind...? I mean... Do you think you could ever...?" Lydia searches for the words she wants to say. "Could we perhaps...?"

"Start again?" Lydia nods. She is right next to me now and leans her body against mine.

"From the beginning?" she asks.

"Well, not quite the beginning." I release Lydia's hand and wrap my arm around her shoulders. "Maybe from where we agree we like each other."

"Oh, right," she says as I pull her to me. "Yes, that would work."

"And maybe we could start at the point where you want me to kiss you."

Lydia relaxes against me. She leans into my body tilting her head back. Her moistened lips slightly parted. She closes her eyes as I trace my finger across her cheek and down her neck. I've waited for this moment. I have dreamed of this moment. Gently, I push a strand of hair from her face as I bend to graze my lips lightly over hers. Lydia sighs and sinks into me further, then I pull away slightly releasing my hold, and look into her eyes. Lydia smiles then reaches her hand around my neck and pulls me to her. We kiss with urgency and desire, enraptured by the moment. Kissing Lydia in real life is even more pleasurable than I imagined it would be. I'm lost in the kiss. The passion. The desire. But we're moving too fast. I break away, find her hands, and hold them in mine. We're both breathing heavily. Both wanting more.

"I'd like to take things slow, if I may, ma'am." I kiss Lydia's fingers. "One step at a time. No need to rush. What do you think?"

"I think you're about the most perfect man in the world. Yes, please. I'd love that."

"Promise me one thing," I say relaxing back against the swing seat which gently rocks to and fro.

"Okay. Although it depends on what the 'one thing' is."

"No more matchmaking. You're not very good at it."

Lydia laughs. "Okay. You're so right. I'll just stick to things that I am good at. Floral design and weddings..."

"And kissing. You're pretty good at kissing."

The moon beams down as I take Lydia in my arms again and kiss her with all my love; with my whole being; with everything that I am. "Taking things slow is going to be difficult," I whisper into her neck.

"It's okay. I won't judge." She kisses me back.

"So, it's late," I say nuzzling Lydia's neck some more. "I could drive you back or..."

Chapter 31

Lydia

Six months later

At Blossom in Bloom, Laura is making a show-stopping Halloween window display from, mostly, crabapples from Luke's ranch. She has arranged them to appear as if the branches are growing on a tree somewhere off to the side. The red, rosy fruit hangs down from the top of the window. A variety of gerbera, daisies, dahlias, and chrysanthemums erupt and explode from rustic metal pails. A pitchfork and a witch's broom complement the Jack o' Lantern sculpted pumpkins in a bed of Fall leaves.

"This is the best display yet," I say with heartfelt commendation giving Laura a grateful squeeze. "I'll take a pic for the website while everything looks dewy fresh. Well done! I'm so lucky to have you." Laura beams at me, proud to have done a fine job.

Marty pops his head out from the workroom out back. "Is it done? Finally?"

"Great works of art take time," says Laura clearing the unused flowers, leaves, and stems away from the window.

I step outside with my phone to take a picture when my attention is grabbed by Sheena who is hurrying toward me down the street.

"Lydia!" she exclaims when she is within earshot. "Guess what?"

"What? I can't guess." But then I can when Sheena waves her hand in my face, showing off a sparkling solitaire diamond ring. "Ha. Congratulations!" We hug on the sidewalk.

"Thanks." Sheena holds up her hand and admires the sparkling ring as if she's seeing it for the very first time. "I'm so excited," she gushes.

"Come in and tell me all about it," I say, genuinely interested in my friend's recent engagement.

"Oh, sorry. I can't just now. But I'll stop by later today because I'd love it if you would design our wedding. It's going to be so beautiful. And perfect." Sheena lets out a little squeal, then she rushes on, past me, down the street. "I'm meeting Gary's parents." She turns and waves. "Wish me luck."

"You don't need luck. They're going to love you."

"Thanks, Lydia. Muah."

Sheena hurries on down the street. I watch her from outside my store for a moment, thinking what an idiot I was not seeing that Sheena is absolutely meant to be with Gary.

I did eventually pluck up the courage to admit my misguided matchmaking scheme to Sheena. I chose my moment and made a special apology bouquet that I took over to her house. She invited me in, and we sat together in her brand-new kitchen. It really is very impressive. Gary has done a great job.

Sheena listened to my confession while our coffee went cold. She didn't say anything for a long time. She just shook her head, occasionally, and looked bewildered.

When I'd finished relating the whole sorry saga, she said, "Gosh, Lydia. This is a real shock. There's a lot to take in."

"Yes, I know," I said, standing up to leave. "I realize that I may have wrecked our friendship, beyond repair. But when you're ready, and if you can, please call me, okay?"

I let myself out.

A few days later, Sheena came to see me at Blossoms in Bloom. She said that, although there was so much wrong with how I went about things, she couldn't be mad at me. She said that the whole episode was just too ridiculous and quite clearly doomed to fail from the start.

"You should write it all down and turn it into a book," she said, laughing and hugging me in the workroom.

I was so relieved and happy to have my friend back, I burst into tears which set Sheena off. We hugged and cried. Then laughed and hugged. Then cried some more.

It turns out that I am not a very competent fairy godmother. And I very nearly blew my own chance of happiness out of the water because of my idiotic ideals and obsessive blinkers. The memory of the calamitous Valentine's Day date still makes me cringe with embarrassment. But I'm getting over it.

I wave to Sheena as she turns the corner and disappears out of sight. She is so happy, and all lit up. It's wonderful to see her glow. Being in love will do that to you. It's the way I feel about Luke. Just thinking about Luke causes a wave of warmth from my toes to my fingertips. Happiness fills me and I feel as if I've turned into gooey caramel. I'm all lit up on the inside.

My thoughts turn to the night Luke and I straightened things out between us. It was so wonderful, I can't help smiling to myself.

I wake up in a strange bed. It takes me a few seconds to reorientate myself and work out where I am. But then a smile spreads across my lips, and I stretch out fully under the bedsheets. I lie there for a while, not wanting to move then, I get up, dress, and go out to find Luke in the stableyard. I guess he'd be up early to check on the newest addition to the Green Acres herd.

Sure enough, Luke leans over the gate and watches as the foal with spindly legs suckles his mother. Treasure makes low contented noises and turns her head to gently lick her baby.

Luke extends his arms to me and pulls me close. He nuzzles my neck. "Good morning. Did you sleep well?"

"Yes. Thank you. The guestroom bed is super comfy." I wrap my arms around Luke's strong lean torso. We stand together holding each other, watching the horse and foal for a few minutes.

Then Luke asks, "Are you hungry? I can make pancakes for breakfast."

"Starving. Yes, to pancakes." I reach my hands up around Luke's neck. "And coffee? I'd love a coffee."

"We have coffee." Luke cups my face in his hands and kisses my lips before reaching for my fingers. We walk together wrapped in each other's arms back to the house.

It's a lovely late spring morning. We enjoy a lavish breakfast on the front porch – blueberry pancakes and a pot of hot strong coffee.

"I'll drive you back to town after breakfast, if you want," Luke says pushing his empty plate away. "I have some errands to run, but no rush."

"Thank you. That would be great." I cut and eat the last slice of pancake dripping in syrup. "I'm glad we decided to take our time. You know." I'm suddenly shy as the memory of the previous night's passion reignites, causing my cheeks to burn. "I'm not going to lie. It was so hard to say goodnight and sleep in the guest room."

"Oh, man. Me too." Luke laughs. "It took all my self-control to be a gentleman last night." Luke sips his coffee. His eyes smile at me over the rim of his cup. "But Lydia. I'd like to go about things the right way." He puts down his coffee cup. "I want to take you out. Go dancing. If you'd like to, we can go horseback riding soon. There are so many pretty trails I want to show you."

"Sounds like I need to schedule some time off," I say leaning toward Luke wanting to kiss him with my syrupy lips.

"We both should, I reckon." Luke smiles his dazzling smile which begins in his blue eyes, the color of a morning sky when you look straight up. "Lydia," he breathes. "You are so so beautiful. Now that we're clear on a few basics, I don't ever want to let you go."

We've been together ever since, enjoying our time together, getting to know each other, naturally, day by day. We talk about the future and what that might bring. But, no rush, we're taking things slow.

The End

ele

If you would like to read another one of Francesca Spencer's fun romcoms, you can find the first two chapters of *Mr Off-limits Grump* on the next page.

What to read next

Mr Off-limits Grump

I'm stuck in a storm with a hot rock star, single dad with no memory before yesterday.

My smalltown café is my whole life.

And I am all done with happily-ever-after.

Or thought I was until Mr Grump walks in.

Scan the QR code with your phone camera then click the link.

Mr Off-limits Grump

Scan here

Start reading on the next page.

1 Jake

I'm driving but don't really know where I'm headed. I just had to drive. Leave L.A. Lah Lah Lah L.A. El Ay. I'm laughing like a crazy person. Los Angeles, the city of angels, huh? I had to put as much distance between me and that place. I don't even know why. If I was being interviewed right now and someone asked, So, what made you run off the stage and keep running, and get into your car, (at least I think it's my car) and drive and keep driving? I wouldn't be able to answer. All I know is I'm driving and I'm getting away. Far away from all that stuff. That music biz stuff. That L.A. stuff. The record company people. The publicity people. The paparazzi with the cameras; the lights; the questions. The fans.

But, no, not the fans. These are the people that gave me everything. Not them. It's the rest of it I can't deal with. I'm exhausted.

I'm a mess. My head is scrambled. I can't think. Am I having a breakdown? Do I need a shrink? Whatdoyacallit? Therapist? Everyone seems to have one these days, huh? But I don't need one because I'm a regular guy, right?

"I'm just a regular guy." That's what I say, isn't it? That is what I said, but am I?

Jeez, I think I'm having some sort of breakdown. I shouldn't have just taken off like that, without even telling Frankie. I know she'll worry. Then she'll hate me. She hates me already. I can hear her now, she's going to say something like, "Dad. This is wacko, even for you!"

The white line on the freeway is hypnotic. Each flash ticks off more distance down the road, but it's making my eyes heavy. Up ahead is a turnoff. I don't even read the name of the town, but it's ten miles away. I hope there's a gas station because the fuel light just came on.

The road winds up a hill, and even though it's dark, I see trees lining either side as I drive past. In the blackness, with my headlights showing up only a few feet of road ahead, I really have to concentrate.

After what seems like forever, streetlights appear around a corner, and, lucky for me, it's a town with a gas station. As I fill up the tank, I take a look around. Across the street, there's an old-style neon sign announcing a hotel that might just be open. I see if they have a room for tonight. It's too late to drive back home now. I need to lie down and close my eyes. This place is so quiet. All I can hear is the buzz of insects and night critters. The lack of sound is soothing like it's massaging my brain.

I'll figure things out, but tomorrow. I'm so tired. I feel like I could sleep for a thousand years.

2 Carly

"Good morning, Sheriff Sullivan. It's a beautiful day." He's in early today and he's pretty pleased with himself too, by the way he swaggered in and stands at the counter with his chest all puffed out like a pigeon.

"Good morning, Carly. Yes, it most certainly is."

I turn to the espresso machine and begin making his coffee. Like most of my regulars, I know what kind of coffee he likes - double shot large cappuccino, extra foam with chocolate.

The bright morning sun bounces off the wooden floor and tables by the window overlooking the yard. I can hear birdsong and the background rush of the river gushing through the gorge below.

I enjoy opening up. The mornings are nearly always quiet mid-week. Just the regulars stop by for their morning caffeine fixes. It's a different story at the weekend. That's when city folk come here for some R and R. It's the quiet that draws them here. And the river, of course.

I place the sheriff's cup on the counter.

"Sully. Call me Sully."

I don't say anything. I smile and nod politely. This is not the first time Sheriff Sullivan has asked me to call him by his nickname, but I would rather keep a professional distance at my place of work.

The Flow Café is not only my place of work, it is my business. It may not be generating the wealth associated with early retirement to a Caribbean Island, but it's a lifestyle choice to be here in sleepy ol' Fairwood. Yep. It's a homey little place that you probably wouldn't come to unless you were into white water rafting, or you wanted to truly get away from it all.

"There's been a report of burglaries in the area." Sheriff Sullivan pauses to sip his coffee. He then licks the foam from his top lip before continuing. Then he places his coffee cup down on the counter and hunts around in his jacket pocket. "Probably a gang, the report says. Targeting holiday places. You know, empty houses like the ones up on the ridge." The sheriff pulls out a folded printout, holding it up for me to see. It shows a blurry image of two guys walking through a glass sliding door, probably taken from CCTV footage. "If you see anyone resembling these

hoodlums, just call me. I'll come right over. No problem."
Sheriff Sullivan puffs out his chest again and tugs up his
pants as he tucks in his shirt. "Just gotta be vigilant. Look
out for each other. Be good neighbors." He says this last
bit as he reaches into his pocket and pulls out some dollars,
which he counts out and slides under his empty cup.

I smile like I always do with Sheriff Sullivan. It's good
to stay on the right side of the local lawman, even if he
thinks he's in with a chance of any kind of romance with
me. Honestly, it gets a little exhausting sometimes. Sheriff
Sullivan is not the only guy in town that comes into The
Flow, dropping hints and flirting like a teenager at a high
school prom. I have become proficient at deflecting un-
wanted romantic attention without losing my profession-
alism. But sometimes I feel like screaming, 'Go away! I have
absolutely no interest in you, you strange little man in uni-
form, with your duck-like feet and your gut spilling over
your belt and that really annoying sniff that punctuates
everything you say!' No. I would never say that. I smile.
I maintain politeness. I have mastered self-possession and
courteous control.

"Well, thank you for letting me know, Sheriff Sullivan.
I will surely keep my eyes open and let you know if I see
anything suspicious."

"I know you will Carly. You are a good citizen, and I can speak for the whole town when I tell you we are glad you decided to stay, even after, you know, everything that happened." He nods at me knowingly, as if we share a secret, which we don't.

Ah yes. Sheriff Sullivan likes to remind me of the one thing I would rather forget. The fact that my fiancé, the person who brought me to Fairwood to open The Flow Café and live out our dream life in this little river community, decided to trade me in for a younger model. Literally.

Brooke, the name of the younger model, was quite simply dazzling, petite, and gorgeous with a highly effective toothpaste commercial smile. She came to Fairwood for a weekend with some gal pals and Conner, my ex-fiancé) took them on a rafting trip, then took her up on her offer of a good time.

It took me a while to recover from the initial shock of finding out the person who was supposed to be my forever mate was actually a man I didn't recognize. How could this person, Conner, who had built a business and a life and made promises to me and convinced me that he was - oh let me see if I can remember the exact words - the happiest man on the planet, just leave with someone in the blink of an eye? At the time, it didn't seem possible. It was a nightmare. He calmly told me that it was a good thing

268

we hadn't gone through with the wedding. Imagine my family all coming over from Ireland to celebrate a sham of a relationship that was doomed to fail.

No. Conner did me a favor. I know that now. He let me keep Rusty, our dog. He was always mine anyway and liked to be in the café, while Conner was guiding on the river. He also let me have the café and all its debt. All he wanted was a quick, clean break. He wasn't going to make things messy for me. He still loved me, he said, and wanted me to be okay. And then he packed a bag, left his key on the kitchen table of our house, and left town. Just like that.

Yes. I was in shock for a long time. But then, slowly, I pulled the broken pieces of my life together. I immersed myself in running a successful business in a beautiful place. I appreciate the good things I have here. I have real friends who care for me. Jodi and Ray were angels after the breakup. They cooked for me and ran the café when I was having a gloomy day and couldn't face the world.

I don't have gloomy days anymore. I don't think about Conner anymore. Not unless someone brings him up in conversation like Sheriff Sullivan did just now. I don't know where Conner is, nor do I care. I have a great life. I really do. Now it's just Rusty and me, I am so happy. Content. Comfortable. Complete. What more could I want?

"Good morning, Carly." Jodi walks in. "And good morning, Sheriff Sullivan," she says with a broad beaming smile. She knows his romantic intentions towards me and thinks it's hilarious that he believes he stands a chance. I tell her I don't know what she's talking about and then she points out that he has never once asked her to call him Sully. "I rest my case," she says, holding up her hands like a courtroom lawyer.

Sheriff Sullivan tips his hat and leaves. More customers come in. A family with three children. A couple dressed in hiking clothes. Jodi and I are busy serving and clearing up. Then we prep for the lunchtime crowd. It's hard to predict just how many customers will come through the door. It's weather dependent, usually. When the sun's out, people feel good and will treat themselves to lunch out at a café or arrange to meet friends for a coffee and a piece of homemade cake. In summer it's pleasant to sit in the shade of the trees on the paved patio out back, where I've planted some raised beds of herbs, salads, and vegetables that I use in the café. Rusty's kennel is tucked around the corner where he likes to snooze most of the day.

The café empties out. Jodi and I chat about her husband Ray, and her kids, Lois and Jim, who are doing well at school. Café work is mostly mundane and repetitive so working with good people keeps things moving along and makes work fun. We have the stereo turned up. Jodi is making sandwiches and I'm unloading the dishwasher. We're singing away to Van Morrison when Jodi stops singing and says, "Oh my. Be still my beating heart."

Scan the QR code to keep reading

Mr Off-limits Grump

Scan here

Thank you!

Writers need readers, so thank you so much for reading my books.

Let's keep in touch.

Visit my Amazon page or find me at

www.francescaspencerauthor.com

I have more fun romcoms coming soon, so make sure you sign up to receive reader offers and updates.

You'll get **Mr Off-limits Grump** to keep for free, plus a little bonus gift.

Loads of love goes out to my fabulous ARC team, my family and, of course, Chloe.

Special thanks and love go out to Frizby, Dany, Sam, Jane, and Megan who welcomed me into their homes, gave me a space to write, and let me help myself to the contents of their fridges. I am forever grateful.

More soon.

x

Francesca Spencer

Laughs, Heart and Happily Ever After

Printed in Great Britain
by Amazon